Christ Hospitality

by Josh Hunt

Hospitality:

An ancient practice that can

refresh your life, revitalize your church and reach your world.

Also by Josh Hunt

You Can Double Your Class in Two Years or Less

Teach Like Jesus

Disciplemaking Teachers (with Dr. Larry Mays)

Enjoying God

Double Services; Double Sunday Schools

You Can Double Your Church in Five Years or Less

One Magnificent Obsession

10 Marks of INCREDIBLE Small Group Leaders

The Amazing Power of Doubling Groups

Copyright © 20012 Josh Hunt

All rights reserved

1964 Sedona Hills Parkway

Las Cruces, NM 88011

575 532 9693

josh@joshhunt.com

Table of Contents

What a Difference One Night Can Make! 3

The Command 22

Friday Night is a Metaphor 42

The Epidemic of Loneliness 69

The Joy of Total Dedication 84

A Heart for People Far From God 109

The Psychology of Influence 131

Epilogue 154

Special Thanks

Special thanks to Missy Hunt, Morgan Malone, and Ted Clee for helping making this a better book.

What a Difference One Night Can Make!

What a difference one night can make. One night can alter the trajectory of your life. One night can redirect your course. One night can undo years of progress or heal years of pain. One night. One night can change eternity.

Progress is rarely a smooth, linear, gradual progression. It nearly always comes in spurts and sputters and delays, then massive growth. All at once all things become new.

It is that way when we drive. Very rarely do you find a highway that bends gradually over a long stretch of road. Usually roads run more or less East or North or whatever for a time, then, all at once we turn and go in a completely different direction. So it is with our walk with God. We run in one direction for a time, then there is a turn that sends us off in a new direction. Not that the first straight stretch of road was a bad one; we needed it to get us to the turn. But the real progress is not in hours of driving but after the turn. We have been driving alongside the mountains for hours and all at once the view radically changes, the air becomes cool and crisp, the aroma of pine causes us to breathe deeply. All at once everything changes.

My life was changed all at once when I went through Henry Blackaby's incredible course, *Experiencing God.* All at once I was awakened to the reality that God is always at work and invites me to join Him in His work. He invites me to join Him in a loving relationship. Following God often involves a crisis of belief, major adjustments and a God-sized vision.

John Piper's *Desiring God* had a similar and sudden effect on me. All at once I realized that a relationship with God was all about enjoying Him. He does not find our desires too strong; he finds them too weak, and our deepest desires are to be satisfied in Him. He is most glorified in us when we are most satisfied in Him.

My life was changed all at once the night I met my wife. Yours likely was too when you met that special someone. All at once my life was totally changed.

My life has been changed a number of times as I have had significant encounters with God. One morning as a six year old child I walked forward to present myself for baptism. I wanted to be on God's team. I didn't know a lot at that young age about what it meant to be a Christian, but I dedicated everything I knew of myself to everything I understood about God. It was a shallow decision in a way, but I think pleasing to God. There is a reason Jesus spoke of coming as a child. All at once, things were different. I didn't know a lot but I did know God had accepted me and I was headed for heaven. All things had become new.

Four years later I had a more profound turning, but again the turn came all at once. Under the influence of some God-anointed preaching I came to a deep conviction about the wrongness of my sin and the darkness of my soul. I wept tears of profound godly sorrow. All at once, everything was different.

It is not hard to come up with biblical examples of this. Let me give you a list of names. See if you can recall a time when their lives were changed all at once. If you are comfortable doing so, write a few notes by each one of these names.

Nicodemus

Moses

Paul

Nehemiah

Peter

Abraham

Blind Bartimaeus

Joseph

Things don't always change all at once. Sometimes they happen gradually. Consider these instructions on how Israel will take the land. Note it is not all at once: "The Lord your God will drive out those nations before you, little by little. You will not be allowed to eliminate them all at once, or the wild animals will multiply around you." Deut. 7:22 (NIV)

Change is not always all at once, but it can be. It is not uncommon. In fact it is the norm.

The First Friday Night

My life was forever changed when we had a couple over to play games one Friday night. We laughed, we played, we enjoyed some homemade coffee cake. Just a normal night of game playing, Diet Coke and coffee cake from one perspective.

From another perspective a night that would change everything. A night that would change forever.

The couple we entertained in our home that Friday night had visited our church the previous Sunday. Like a lot of churches we had quite a few visitors, but not many of them stayed around. As I explain in *You Can Double Your Church in Five Years or Less* we had a high magnet factor (how many visitors the church attracts) and a low velcro factor (how many visitors join).

We had been in the habit of having some friends over on a Friday night. This was not part of some global strategy to win the world to Jesus, although it has turned into one.

Somewhere along the line I had picked up on the fact that, all things being equal, the quicker you contact Sunday morning visitors the more effective the contact. Monday is better than Tuesday. Tuesday is better than Wednesday. And, if you wait three weeks before calling them it is almost impossible to persuade people that you are *really* glad they came. So, following this line of thought, I made my calls on Sunday afternoon–the quicker the better.

So, I called this particular couple and I said the same things to them that I said to other visitors I had called in the past– "How did you hear about our church? What kind of work are you in? How long have you lived here? What kind of churches have you attended in the past?" and so forth. I have some introvert in me and so it helps me to have a few questions prepared to keep the conversation going. Then, I said these magic words, "We are going to have some friends over to our home this Friday night, and we were wondering if you might like to join us. It will be an informal thing, no big program or event. We are just going to hang out, have Diet Coke, coffee cake and play some cards." To my surprise and delight, he said, "Sure. Sounds fun. Can we bring something?" "Key lime pie is what I am feeling, if you are taking requests!" (I don't actually say that about the key lime pie, but I will let them bring something.)

That Friday night our new friends showed up. We did not get out a flip chart and go over sixteen reasons to believe in the existence of God. We did not have a PowerPoint prepared on common objections to the gospel and answers to each one of those objections. We just hung out, had Diet Coke, played table games and enjoyed some coffee cake.

I might add that during the eleven years I served on staff as the minister of education in the church we were attending at this time, we enjoyed eleven consecutive years of growth. We grew from one service and one Sunday School to four services and four Sunday Schools, including a Saturday night service and "Sunday School." The group that came to our home on Friday nights attended the Saturday night service and "Sunday School." (We didn't actually call it Sunday School since it met on Saturday night.)

The Saturday night after enjoying a night of fun and fellowship in our home on Friday, that couple were in church. Not only did they come to church, they stayed for the Bible study that followed. We were on our way to becoming friends. That one night made all the difference.

They came back the next week and the next and the next and the next. In virtually every church service I have been in, whether the pastor is preaching on how to win over worry, how to raise your kids, or how to pray, it is a common thing that the pastor will explain, in a brief way, how to become a Christian. So, over the next several weeks, this couple heard the gospel message not one time, but several times. About a month later, they placed their faith in Christ. I had the privilege of baptizing both of them.

We had another couple over and they joined the church. We had another couple over and they joined the church. We had another couple over and they joined the church.

To be fair, only about a fourth of these were coming placing their faith in Christ. The rest were coming as Baptists who had moved to town from Alabama. One parenthetical note: some people who do what I do come close to saying that there is no redeeming value in reaching Baptists who move to town from Alabama. I take a contrarian viewpoint. I think it is a good thing to reach Baptists who move to town from Alabama. I think God loves Baptists who move to town from Alabama. I think God wants Baptists who move to town from Alabama in church and growing as disciples. It is a good thing. We ought to pay some attention to whether they are the *only* people we are reaching, but it is a good thing to reach them. I have been in some fat, happy churches in the South that are growing by 15% a year, yet baptize half the national average for their size of church. You can do this by just reaching Baptists who move to town from Alabama. (A good rule of thumb is this: the average church baptizes 10% of the attendance each year. Try to be above average.)

After six months of inviting church visitors into our home on Friday nights, I decided to do some research. I discovered forty-three couples had visited our church who would have been prospects for this particular Saturday night Bible study class. Of these forty-three, we had entertained ten in our home. Thirty-three we did not have into our home. We did this every couple of weeks and all you can do is all you can do. Of the thirty-three we did not have in our home, three joined the church.

I didn't know this at the time, but this is just about the national average. I did a survey where I asked five hundred churches:

- How many visit your church?
- How many join your church?
- How many attend your church?
- How many attended a year ago?

Based on the input from five hundred churches, I discovered that our numbers where just about the national average. On average, 87% of the people who visit our churches do not join those churches. You see, we think our problem is we can't get people to come to church. That is, in fact, not our problem. Our problem is not that we can't get them to come to church. Our problem is they have been to church. And, in many cases they don't want to come back.

The question is, does coffee cake really make a difference? Does it make a quantifiable difference that you can actually see? Well, look carefully at the chart above. It is the blue slice we are interested in. That is the number of people who joined without coffee cake. With coffee cake, the blue slice looks like the second chart.

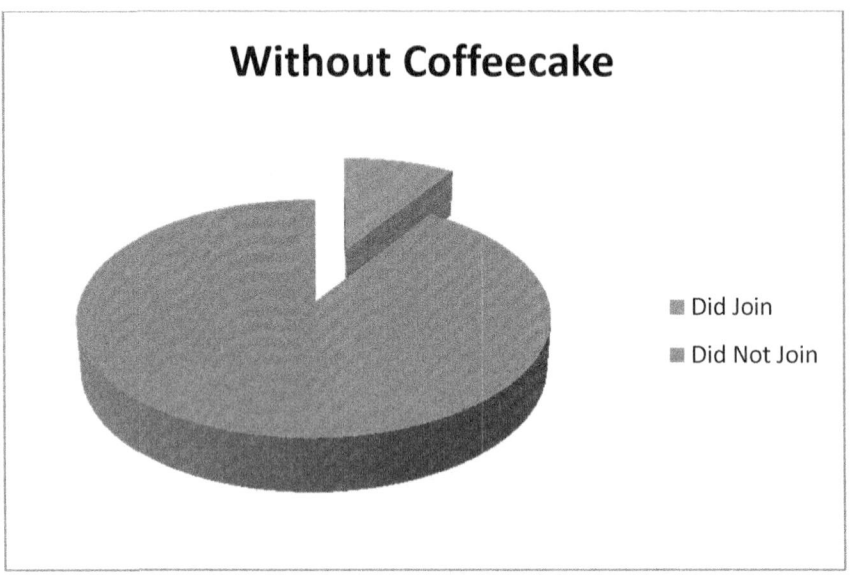

Same pastor, same church, same music, same preschool, same order of worship, same landscaping, same building. The only difference was the coffee cake.

Some people ask me, "What do you put in that coffee cake?" What you put in that coffee cake is L.O.V.E. You love people in common, ordinary, pedestrian ways and their heart will begin to warm up to a message about a God who loves them. All at once, things will start changing. If you will be their friend, their heart will warm up to a message about, "What a friend we have in Jesus."

What a difference one night can make.

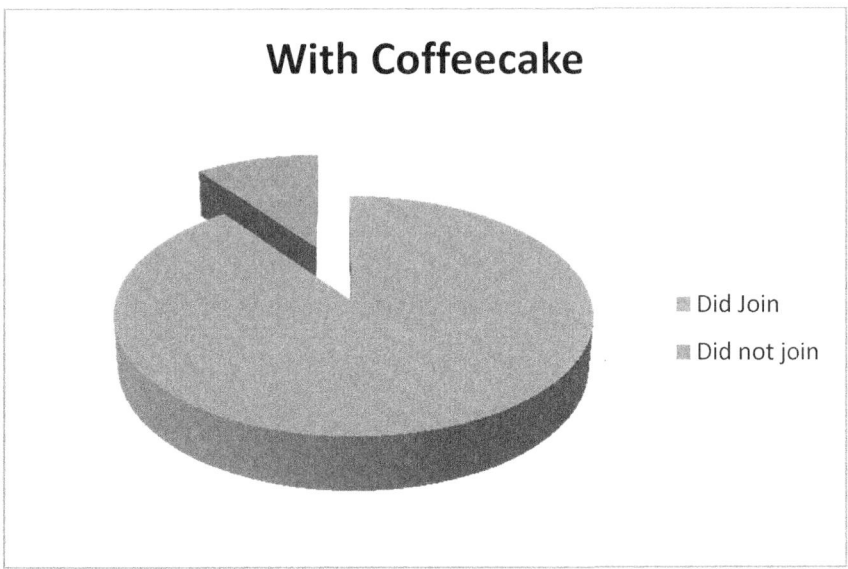

The reason is, as Rick Warren puts it, "People are not looking for a friendly church; they are looking for friends." A guy at our local mall helped me to understand the difference. He was working at one of those little kiosks selling electronic gizmos and gadgets. He surprised me when he called me by name. He didn't look even vaguely familiar to me.

"Are you Josh Hunt?" he asked.

"I am sorry; you have me at a bit of an advantage. I am sure I should remember your name, but I am really spacey," I replied.

"Oh, I wouldn't expect you to remember me. I used to attend your church but I don't attend church anymore," he said. Then he really surprised me. He asked, "Would you like to know why? Would you like to know why I don't attend church anymore?"

Let me ask you the same question: Would you like to know why? Would you like to know the reason why this guy doesn't attend church anymore?

Very bluntly stated he said, "People are only nice to you at church."

It wasn't enough for him. It wasn't enough that we declared a message about a God who loved him. He wanted people to love him too. It wasn't enough that we told him about how he could have a friend in Jesus. He wanted human friends as well. It is not enough to just deliver content about a God who loves; we must represent God. That is, we must help people to feel from us what God feels about them–love.

I used to talk about *Giving Friday Nights to Jesus* based on my own experience. But, I have presented this message to hundreds of churches all across America. I will do my third tour of Australia this year. I will do a hundred and twenty conferences this year and have been presenting this message full time for eight years. And, I am getting really positive feedback.

I had a guy in Florida tell me, "I am hitting 100%. Every single person I have had into my home and fed my coffee cake to has joined my church." Now, I don't want to be critical, but Floridians don't exactly have the most proven track record when it comes to counting, so I am a little suspicious. But, he could be off quite a bit and still this would be an impressive number.

Another guy in Ohio told me he is getting 87%. Eighty-seven percent of the people he had in his home and fed his coffee cake to joined his church. He grew his church from 100 to 1100 in seven years using this strategy. Another guy in Oklahoma told me 90%. Another guy in California told me, "nine out of ten." Same pastor, same sermons, same music, same everything; the only difference was the coffee cake.

Someone has said, "People come to church for a thousand different reasons but they only stick around for one: friends." They don't stick around because of the eloquence of the pastor. They don't stick around because of the beauty of the choir or because the church has a hot band. They stick around because someone scribbles their name on the back of their phone book. Someone gets their phone number entered into their cell phone. Someone at church becomes their friend.

It Doesn't Work Everywhere

It doesn't work everywhere. Let me tell you some stories where it doesn't work to help you to clarify how it can.

One guy said to me, "I love your book. I love your ideas. I especially love the idea of giving Friday night to Jesus. Love that idea."

"How is it working?" I asked. I am always curious to hear another success story.

"Oh, I don't do it; I just think it is a great idea." It wasn't working in his case.

Another guy came to me and said, "I don't think it will work in my case."

"Really? Why not?" I quizzed.

"I don't really like to do anything." he answered.

"Come on, there has got to be some things you like to do. Think about it." I said.

 "Nope. I don't really like to do anything. And, what is more, I am married to a very boring woman. She doesn't like to do anything either. We are just two happy little clams staying home doing nothing together," he stated.

 I pushed him further. "Come on, now, there has to be something you like to do."

"Well, now that you push me, I can think of one thing. Once a year we like to go into the city and attend the opera." Opera. How are you doing with opera? Do you like opera? Do you like opera well enough to have paid money to attend in the last twelve months? I didn't think so. I am told about 2% of the population enjoys opera music. So, this guy's situation is, once a year he likes to do what 2% of the population enjoys. In light of that fact, I told him, "You better get a visitation program going. Hire an evangelist. Put on a crusade. Get on T.V. There are a lot of ways you can do evangelism. I don't think this one is going to work for you."

It doesn't work for everyone.

I had a lady ask, "How can this work with my ladies? I minister to 85-year-olds and up shut-ins?"

I am thinking, "If they are truly shut-ins, I don't think it will work for you." (I have heard ministers complain about the fact that when they call on shut-ins, they are never home. It might work with those shut-ins.)

I had a man say to me, "I work with prisoners. How can this work for me?"

I am thinking, "Not so well." Call Chuck Colson. He knows a lot about prison ministry. I don't think this is going to work in your context. It doesn't work everywhere.

It Doesn't Work Every Time

There is not a one-to-one relationship between every invitation and every time people respond. There is not a one-to-one relationship between every time they come to the party and every time they get involved in the class. There is not a one-to-one relationship, but it happens often enough to make a huge difference. One night really can make a huge difference.

I remember one time inviting four couples who had visited our church to join us on a Friday night. I called all four couples on Monday night and all four said they would join us. I called on Thursday night to confirm. Four couples confirmed that they would be there.

Now, I might explain that when we have people over, my wife likes to have the house clean. She likes to have the living room clean, the kitchen clean, the bathroom clean, the dining room clean, the bedroom clean, the bedroom bathroom clean, and the bedroom bathroom shower clean. I have explained this to her: "They are not going to take a shower."

I don't want to overstate the case here, but when we have people over, I try to do my fair share. So, on Friday afternoon, I am buying the Diet Coke, making the coffee cake, vacuuming the floor and, of course, cleaning the shower.

The party was schedule to start at 7:00. On schedule, our friends showed up. We were enjoying some Diet Coke, coffee cake and table games, but in the back of my mind, I am thinking, "What happened to all our visitor couples?" None of the four couples that I had invited on Monday and had confirmed on Thursday showed up. None.

I called this one guy; Ron was his name. "Ron, where are you?" (I was probably not filled with the Spirit at this moment!)

"Oh, I got off work, I was tired, my work is a hassle and I just didn't feel like getting out tonight," he replied.

"Ron, you need to come over and see my bathroom, man. I have been shining this thing up, just for you!" I didn't actually say that, but I wanted to. It will happen to you.

It doesn't work every single time, but it will work often enough to make a huge difference. One night really can make a huge difference.

The Command

Several times in my life I have discovered something someplace other than the Bible, then turned to see what the Bible had to say about it. Sure enough, it was there all the time. This was true in this case. If I had eyes to see, I could have discovered this through reading the Bible. It was there all along.

Get in the habit

Romans 12.13 says, "Get in the habit of inviting guests home for dinner." [NLT] Notice two things about this verse. First, what kind of language do you find here? Is this a parable or a proverb or a prophecy or apocalyptic literature or what? English students will find this an easy question. It is a command. As surely as God has commanded us to pray or give or serve or read our Bibles or attend church, our sovereign God has commanded us to, "Get in the habit of inviting guests home for dinner." It is a command.

Someone asked me once, "What is the hardest thing you have to communicate?" By far and away the hardest thing I have to communicate is to get people to get serious about having fun. I struggle to communicate that this is a serious issue. It sounds so light and fluffy. It sounds so fun. It sounds a bit trivial. It doesn't sound important, the stuff of dedication and commitment and kingdom work. But it is. It is serious business because it is about love expressed in a very practical, tangible way. There is a reason God has commanded this.

Note also, it is a command to "Get in the habit." Researchers say about 90% of our behavior is habitual. We have a habit for brushing our teeth, driving to work, packing our bags, scrambling an omelet, and so forth. The same with inviting guests home for dinner. It is either a habit, and we do it regularly, or it is not, and it has been a long time sense a guest had their feet under our table. We don't do it at all. God's command is to get in the habit.

Offer hospitality without grumbling

Again: notice what kind of language this is: "Offer hospitality to one another without grumbling." 1 Peter 4:9 [NIV] Again, it is a command. As surely as God has commanded us to pray or attend church or read the Bible he has commanded us to offer hospitality without grumbling. If we will be obedient to the command of God to offer hospitality without grumbling, we can have an amazing impact on our world.

Notice, the command is to offer. I hope this book will fire you up to do just that. I hope you will do something about what you read. Not just being a hearer of the word, but a doer also (James 1.23) You might find yourself saying, "I am going to do it. I am going to have some people over to my house to enjoy a meal together." I don't want to pop your bubble, and I do appreciate your enthusiasm. But, you don't actually know if you will or not. You can't control whether or not you will have people over. All you can control is the offer. Offer hospitality without grumbling. All you can do is offer. Sometimes they will say yes. Sometimes they will say no. Sometimes they will say they will come and they won't. Occasionally they will pop in on you when they told you they couldn't be there. You can't control whether they come. All you can control is whether you offer.

Sometimes you will offer and offer and offer and offer and people won't respond for a long time. Keep offering. One time, I had offered and offered and offered. Maybe a dozen times. They always had a nice tone and seemed interested, but they didn't come. I kept offering. After a while, it occurred to me that I might be misreading their tone. They might not be the least bit interested but are just too polite to say anything. I am a believer in English language sentences as a primary means of communication. Some people are into subtleties of body language and tone and hints; I am more into English language sentences. Perhaps it is the writer in me.

So I said to them, "Say, I have invited you guys to a number of things, and you always sound interested but you never come. It occurs to me I may be misreading you. If you are not interested, just let me know and I will quit calling." "Oh no, we love to turn you down! Keep right on calling." I don't remember about that couple, but I know that with some couples, they turned me down a half a dozen times or more, but later got very involved in the church.

I asked this one guy about this later. "What took you guys so long to come around? What took you guys so long to respond?" "You know," he reflected, "Every time you would call I would turn to my wife and say, 'That is Josh again. They have a pizza party coming up. We really should get involved one of these days.'" Get involved. Not come to pizza. Get involved. He understood I was not inviting him to pizza, I was inviting him to be in the church. I was inviting him to be a part of community. I was inviting him to be my friend. He wasn't quite ready.

Rick Warren says it takes 18 miles in the open ocean to turn an oil tanker around. Eighteen miles. It takes a long time to turn some lives around, too. Andy Stanley is fond of saying, "Think steps, not programs." Step one was to show up at church. He had to get comfortable with that step before he was ready to go onto step two. After a few months, he did respond to an invitation to come to a party. He accepted the offer. A little while after that, he came to class. Then, he started to attend class regularly. Then he got really involved–reading his Bible, getting in discipleship groups, discovering his spiritual gifts and so forth. But, one step at a time.

Some churches have what I like to call a "pounce strategy" for handling visitors. They pounce on them as soon as they visit. "Seven touches in seven days," that is the motto of some churches. A call today, an email tomorrow, a visit the next day, a pastoral contact, a Sunday School contact, a card, and so forth. Great. That is all well and good. Nothing wrong with that strategy, unless you come off as desperate for members, like a guy who tries too hard to get a date. Still, not a bad strategy and better than the more common strategy of ignoring visitors.

The question is, what do you do the second week and the second month and the sixth month? The vast majority of churches have no strategy whatsoever for contacting visitors after the first week or two. But, it takes 18 miles in the open ocean to turn an oil tanker around. And it takes a long time to turn a life around. If we don't have a strategy for personally (underline that last word, will you?) contacting visitors over the next year, we will miss out on an opportunity to impact their lives.

The command to offer hospitality gives us the opportunity to do just that. The nice thing about this strategy is it does not get old. If you call someone and invite them to group and they don't come and you call them again and they don't come and you call them again and they don't come, pretty soon it will get pretty darn awkward. If you are not careful, you will end up representing a message that is contrary to the message of the gospel itself. The gospel is all about the idea that, "There is therefore now NO condemnation for those in Christ." Romans 8.1 We preach a no condemnation gospel or we are not preaching Christ's gospel at all. It is not about a balance between a little bit of condemnation and a little bit of grace. It is about no condemnation. But, if we invite people and they don't come, invite them and they don't come, and invite them and they don't come, before long we will begin to represent condemnation. We will come off as a policeman who caught them not doing the right thing. But, if we invite them to a party once a month, that is just being hospitable. That is just being friendly. It is not about condemnation. It is about being friends.

The third thing I would like for you to notice about this verse is that it says, "Offer hospitality *without grumbling.*" Let me explain what that means. For one thing, it means, sometimes you will invite them and they won't come. We looked at that. Sometimes they will say they will come and they won't come. We looked at that as well. Sometimes, when they come, they will drive you nuts.

Let's say you go to a pot-luck dinner. You have the common decency–and it just seems like that to you; nothing heroic, just common decency–to bring a big casserole or two large pizzas or a big bucket of chicken. Emphasis on the words, "large" and "big." The point is, you have the decency to bring enough for your family and about that much more. But, somewhere along the line you will offer hospitality and you will notice that a family of six, with four strapping teenage boys will come in with one small bag of Doritos. Again, it is probably not the most spiritual part of me that notices this kind of thing, but I have.

Let's say you host the pot-luck dinner. You have the decency, if you go to someone's house for a pot-luck, to help with the dishes afterwards. They may gently resist your offer, but you will have none of it. Next thing you know your arms are elbow deep in the dishwater and before long the kitchen shines like a 409 commercial. But, you will have some people over, and they don't have that common decency. You will enjoy dinner, then maybe slip to the living room to do what we have done many times: dinner and a movie. Pot-luck dinner at 6.00, movie at 7.00.

After the movie, the group will linger for a time in lively conversation, heading home about 10.30 or so. You start to head for bed, but then take a glance into the kitchen. It is piled to the ceiling with dishes. Now, you may be one of these people who cannot sleep with dirty dishes in the kitchen. (I must say I am at a bit of an advantage here. I can sleep just fine with dirty dishes in the sink. I had a friend who told me that after years of marriage, his wife has never gone to bed with dirty dishes in the sink. I thought, "My dishes don't always make it to the sink, either." I don't think that is what he meant.)

So, at 11.00 at night, you are doing dishes, mumbling and grumbling the whole time. I want to remind you of what the good Book says: Offer hospitality without grumbling.

Work together

"We ought therefore to show hospitality to such men so that we may work together for the truth." 3 John 1:8 [NIV]

What is the nature of this language: show hospitality? Is it a proverb, a parable, a promise, or what? Again, it is a command. God is commanding us to show hospitality. A surely as He has commanded us to pray or give, He has commanded us to show hospitality.

Note also it says, "so that we may work together." Work together. Evangelism is done best as a team. Ministry is not a solo sport, but a team sport. Teamwork makes the dream work.

I have discovered, that as a category, teachers are not the funnest people in our churches. Teachers, well, their idea of a good time is hanging out at Barnes and Noble for the evening. Not exactly exciting entertainment for most, but that is what teachers like to do. I know that because I am a teacher. My idea of a good time is hanging out at Barnes and Noble for the evening. A lot of people assume that because I teach a party-driven strategy, that I am an extroverted, fun-loving, out-going kind of guy. It is actually not true of me. I am actually rather introverted. I believe in the party-driven strategy because I have seen it work, and because I believe God has commanded it. Many of us who have gifts of teaching are not naturally gregarious, winsome, people-people. We need a team of people surrounding us so we may work together for the truth.

Every church has a slightly different spin on how a group ought to be organized. I don't have a particular bias for one team set-up over another. Some have larger classes and small care groups. In some cases the care groups actually meet on a weekly basis, while in others they are just "paper" groups. That is, they are organizational units with someone in charge who keeps up with the group members, but they don't actually meet together. Some go with small groups, organized in department structures. Some churches have smaller, independent groups.

Within the group, there are various officers that are used. Inreach leaders, outreach leaders, fellowship leaders, hospitality leaders, greeters, administrative leaders, and prayer leaders are common examples of team members.

I was in a group once that organized around L.O.T. Leaders (Leaders of Ten), based on Jethro's conversation with Moses where he says, get leaders of thousands, hundreds, fifties and tens. Each Leader of Ten had a list of approximately ten people that they were to call and invite to parties. Some of the ten were regular attenders, some were absentees, some were prospects.

Team members can be selected in a variety of ways. One way I have seen work is to have an "election day" once a quarter. On the first week of the quarter, talk about goals of the group, and who would like to do what. Hold an election to elect officers for the quarter. The election is rather informal and consists mostly of taking volunteers and affirming one another's giftedness to do certain tasks. It also allows a polite exit for people who are not well suited for what they were assigned the previous semester.

The key member of the team is what we call the class President. I have heard terms like class leader, or even evangelism director, although leader is more descriptive. If you have someone who caries a Palm or Pocket PC, they make an ideal candidate for this position. Those of us who carry a Palm, we don't tend to do any real work—we just delegate and supervise and manage and oversee. You might be tempted to ask someone to do this who has the gift of service, because they are so willing to help. However, someone with the gift of service is hard wired to serve. So, as they think about an upcoming party, they go over all the details in their mind. They think, "I could get Mary to bring drinks, Bob and Gill to bring chips, and Barbara and Tom to bring dessert. Let's see, George would be good at calling outsiders, Sandra would do well at calling people in the class. Let' see, Brenda, Kathy and Sue always do well with decorations and seem to enjoy it. . . You know, I don't need to trouble all of them; I can just do it all myself!" People who carry a Palm, who tend to have a gift for administration, don't suffer from this kind of dilemma. They realize it is work getting other people to work. It is work calling and asking, and getting back with people and checking on them and inspecting what you expect. It is all work. They are happy to do it; they are gifted for it. But, they realize it is work. It is their part of the work.

My favorite Old Testament book is Nehemiah. Chapter three looks like one of the more boring chapters in the Bible, but it contains the secret to Nehemiah's success. Notice the underlined phrases.

- Meremoth son of Uriah, the son of Hakkoz, <u>repaired the next section</u>. <u>Next to him</u> Meshullam son of

Berekiah, the son of Meshezabel, made repairs, and <u>next to him</u> Zadok son of Baana also made repairs. Neh. 3:4 [NIV]

- <u>Adjoining this</u>, Jedaiah son of Harumaph made repairs opposite his house, and Hattush son of Hashabneiah made repairs <u>next to him</u>. Neh. 3:10 [NIV]
- <u>Next to him</u>, the repairs were made by the Levites under Rehum son of Bani. <u>Beside him</u>, Hashabiah, ruler of half the district of Keilah, carried out repairs for his district.
- <u>Next to him</u>, the repairs were made by their countrymen under Binnui son of Henadad, ruler of the other half-district of Keilah. Neh. 3:17-18 [NIV]

Next to him, next to him, next to him. This is how we can be effective for God. Teamwork makes the dream work.

What a concept: the teachers teach, the leaders lead, the encouragers encourage, the planners plan, the servers serve, the mercy givers give mercy. Work together for the truth. Don't attempt to do the work of ten men; get ten men (or women) to do the work.

We have looked at three commands so far:

- A command to get in the habit of inviting guests home for dinner.

- A command to offer hospitality without grumbling.
- A command to do hospitality as a team.

This raises a question: who are we to invite to these hospitality events? You might be surprised to learn that Jesus answered this question very specifically. His answer might surprise you.

Who to invite

Let's play a little game. See if you can find the difference between how these two translations treat this verse. Hint: one translation adds a word not found in the other one.

- Then he told the man who had invited him, "When you invite people for lunch or dinner, don't invite only your friends." Luke 14:12 (GW)
- Then Jesus said to his host, "When you give a luncheon or dinner, do not invite your friends." Luke 14:12 [NIV]

There may be other differences, but I noticed this one. In God's Word translation, the translators inserted the word "only." "Don't invite *only* your friends." You don't find it in the NIV, nor any other mainline translation, nor would you find it in the Greek. Why did the translators of God's Word put it in?

I took every Greek class available to me except one. I don't know enough Greek to do any actual translating, but I do have a feel for how translators think. I think the conversation went something like this. "It seems kind of unthinkable that Jesus would actually forbid people from asking their friends over for dinner. It just seems a little un-Jesus-like to declare it a sin that we would ever have some friends over to the house for pizza. Could it be there is another reasonable explanation?"

The Bible is not written in lawyer-ese. It is written in the language of the street. It is called Koine Greek, meaning, common Greek. It is written the way we normally talk. It is not a technical manual, but rather the real recording of every day speech. In everyday speech, when we want to strengthen a point–to say it really loudly, if you will–we often employ a common verbal device called a hyperbole. If you are a little rusty on your English, don't let it scare you. It is an exaggeration to make a point. It is not a lie; it is an exaggeration to make a point, and everyone listening knows it as such. Suppose I said, "Everyone was at the concert!" or, "The whole city turned out for the parade." What would you take that to mean? Everyone or a bunch of people? The whole city, or a big crowd? We use hyperbole all the time to make a point.

The translators of God's Word seemed to think that Jesus is using a hyperbole here to strengthen His point. And, I think they are right. It does seem kind of un-Jesus-like that Jesus would forbid people from inviting friends over for a pizza. So, I agree with the translators. But, my point in bringing this out is that Jesus is saying this in spades. He is screaming. He is underlining his point and putting it in a bold face font.

"How could you think of ever having a get-together and not inviting some people who are far from God? How could you entertain the idea of entertaining friends and not including outsiders in the circle? Are you going to put together a golf foursome? Don't fill up the foursome with your church buddies. Make it a threesome, and discipline yourself to make that last member someone who is a prospect for your group, or an absentee from your class."

I have seen it happen more times than I can count, if we can get them to the party, we wouldn't be able to keep them from class.

It happened for us just recently. My wife and I are currently teaching the college class at our church. I say my wife and I, it is mostly my wife. I am traveling speaking about 40 Sundays a year. We try to work her schedule so she is gone not more than one Sunday a month. Recently we had a Christmas party for the students. Christmas break was right after that, but the next week when everyone was back, my wife called me in Florida. "We had a new guy there today, one of the ones that came to that Christmas party." I have seen it happen more times than I can count; if you can get them to the party you couldn't keep them from class.

The Levi Plan

As you read this passage: look for Levi's strategy for reaching his office for Christ:

> After this, Jesus went out and saw a tax collector by the name of Levi sitting at his tax booth. "Follow me," Jesus said to him, and Levi got up, left everything and followed him.
> Then Levi held a great banquet for Jesus at his house, and a large crowd of tax collectors and others were eating with them. But the Pharisees and the teachers of the law who belonged to their sect complained to his disciples, "Why do you eat and drink with tax collectors and 'sinners'?"

> Jesus answered them, "It is not the healthy who need a doctor, but the sick. I have not come to call the righteous, but sinners to repentance." Luke 5:27-32 [NIV]

There is within the heart of anyone who has ever been touched by grace and inclination that says, "I have got to tell someone!" In a way it is a spiritual inclination, in a way it is just a human inclination. In a way it is true of any good news that comes our way. Whether it is the birth of a new grand-baby or the opening of a new Wal-mart, when good news comes our way, we want to tell someone.

I remember when my third child (and first daughter) was born I had an especially strong inclination to walk up to anyone who would hear me and say, "We had a baby!" I remember buying some gas just after Destiny was born. I wanted to get a box and stand outside the gas station and say to anyone who would listen: "We had a baby!" But I didn't. And the reason might be a little obscure to you. Because I speak for a living, you might think I am a naturally extroverted, stand-on-a-box kind of guy. You might think that, but you would be wrong. I am actually pretty introverted. And, although I felt something deeply about my joy in having a baby girl, I struggled to find a way to communicate it.

Many of us struggle to find a way to communicate our joy in God. Research indicates that about 90% of Christians struggle with evangelism. We take the training and learn the verses and study the outlines and prepare our testimony but we still struggle. It can hardly be trained out of us. Most of us struggle with evangelism. That is why a book with at title like, *I Hate Witnessing* can resonate with so many. A lot of us feel that way.

I think Levi felt this way the day he decided to throw a party. I think he thought, "How can I get this message about Jesus down to those beer-drinking, fun-loving, dirty-joke-telling coworkers at the I.R.S. office," where Levi worked. Perhaps he thought about holding a crusade. Perhaps he thought about organizing a visitation program. Perhaps he thought about passing out tracts. We don't know what he thought about, but we do know what he came up with. Levi threw a party. Levi was the first one to give Friday nights to Jesus. And I get the impression some of his co-workers became followers of Christ because of Levi's expression of hospitality.

"I was a stranger"

Jesus took the idea of entertaining strangers very seriously, and we should too. He said that when we entertain strangers, it is like we are entertaining Jesus.

Think about that next time you give Friday nights to Jesus. This is not just about coffee cake and game playing and Diet Coke. It is about entertaining Jesus.

In Matthew 25.35, Jesus says, "I was a stranger and you invited me in." If every church would treat every visitor like they really were Jesus, we wouldn't have a church growth problem in America. That is what it comes down to: being like Jesus by treating people like Jesus.

Friday Night is a Metaphor

Friday Night is a metaphor. It doesn't have to be Friday night. This may seem like an obvious point, but I have had a number of people miss this. They say something to me like this. "Uh, Brother Hunt, I don't think this is going to work out in my case." "Oh really, why not?" "Well, my son marches in the marching band." "And. . ." "Well, they have football games on Friday night." "And. . ." "And my son marches at the half-time of the football games." "And. . ." "I feel I should support my son by going to the football games on Friday night, so I can't do this Friday night for Jesus thing."

It doesn't have to be Friday night. Friday night is a metaphor.

Pizza on Sunday

It could be Pizza on Sunday. True story of a Sunday School teacher in Missouri named Chris. He grew his class, the first time I met from 4 to 40 in nine months. How did he do it? Pizza on Sunday. Then, I came back a second time. He had just started a new class–he and his wife and two other couples. I asked him to check in with me, "When you get this group doubled, send me an email." Six months later, he sent me an email. "Just checking in. Next month we will send out 25 people to start a new class. We will have 35 in our class." He went from 6 to 60 in 6 months. How did he do it? Pizza on Sunday.

He called me last summer. "I am back up to 40 again. I want to divide my class, but here is the deal. We are having a hard time finding preschool and children's workers." (Sound familiar?) "So, here is what I want to do. Instead of sending ten people out to start a new class, I am sending ten people out help in the preschool and children's area to teach. Do you think that is a good idea? Do you think it is OK that I delay starting a class to do this?" I think it is a great idea. How did Chris do it? What was his plan? Pizza on Sunday.

This is what you will need to do. I will tell you a lot of ideas about how to give Friday nights to Jesus. Along the way, be thinking of ideas of your own–things that you like to do. What you need to do is translate my details of pizza on Sunday or Chinese food on Sunday night, (we will get to that soon), through the lens of the metaphor of giving Friday nights to Jesus and out the other side come details of your own.

One church that has done this in spades in New Life Community Church in Colorado Springs. Pastor Ted

Haggard has written up their strategy in a book called *Dog Training, Fly Fishing and Sharing Christ*. They have hundreds of groups all over Colorado Springs. Ted says the curious thing is that many people who are in their groups don't even know they are in a New Life Group. They think there are in a dog training group, or a fly fishing group. What they don't realize is New Life has sent a missionary to that group and trained that missionary to move people one step closer to Christ each semester.

New Life has carefully defined what this means, and has provided strategies to move people down what is called the Engle Scale. The Engle Scale has a mid point of "0" that represents coming to Christ. Everything on the right side of the scale is discipleship. On the extreme left side of the scale is, "No knowledge of God whatsoever." Then, they have set up baby steps from that point to becoming a Christian and beyond. The scale looks like this:

Level	Description
-12	No God framework
-11	Experience of emptiness
-10	God framework
-9	Vague awareness and belief in God
-8	Wondering if God can be known
-7	Aware of Jesus
-6	Interested in Jesus
-5	Experience of Christian love
-4	Aware of the basic facts of the gospel
-3	Aware of personal need
-2	Grasp the implications of the gospel
-1	Challenged to respond personally
0	Repentance and faith
+1	Holy Spirit and baptism
+2	Functioning member of local Church
+3	Continuing growth in character,
+4	Part of Team Leadership

The goal: to move people one step closer to Christ each semester starting with where people are and the connection point of dog training of fly fishing. Is it working? In spades.

Back to Chris's story. What is working for Chris is doing what a lot of pastors do. He wanders around the auditorium and glad-hands with people. Doing this week by week he knows who the visitors are, and who the members are. He shakes hands, connects, says "hi" and is just generally friendly. When he finds a visitor that might be a prospect for his class, he pauses. He talks a little longer. He asks about the kids. Then he says these magic words, "Say, listen, a bunch of us are going to go get pizza after while. If you would like, we would love to have you come along. I am buying the pizza! Do you think you might could join us?"

That is his strategy. Pizza on Sunday. Sounds simple enough, but it grew his class from 4 to 40 in 9 months and 6 to 60 in 6 months. If you love them they will come to love our Lord. If you will be their friend, their heart will warm up to a message about what a friend we can have in Jesus.

Chris has never given a single, solitary Friday night to Jesus in the literal sense of Friday night. What he did was to ask himself, "What do I like to do?" and build that into a ministry. That is what a group in California did as well.

Chinese food on Sunday night

Another true story. This is a church in California. I have been there three times over about a five year period of time.

The first time I was there the pastor asked me after the evening service if I wanted to go out for Chinese food with a group. I said that sounded fun.

It didn't take long to observe that this group had a tradition. Everyone seemed to know what to do except me. They all ordered off the menu, got one helping of their entré, then set their entré out in the middle of the table and ate family style, enjoying a little from a variety of Chinese dishes. As we sat there a guy across the table talked about a computer he just bought. Another guy talked about an RV he was thinking about buying. A lady got out pictures of her grand kids. (This was a group of middle-aged adults.) I challenged them to invite every member and every prospect to Chinese food once a month. They already had the fellowship. All they had to do was build it into a ministry. I came back to that same church 6 months later to discover that attendance was up by 100–a 33% increase in 6 months because they took what they enjoyed doing and built it into a ministry. I came back again five years later and found them still growing. Their strategy: Chinese food on Sunday night.

It doesn't have to be big and elaborate

I love this story because it illustrates something else about this ministry: it doesn't have to be big and elaborate. It can be rather simple.

Some people like doing big and elaborate. They like to do progressive dinners where you go to the North side of the county and have salad, go to the South side of town and have bread, go out West and have vegetables, and on to the East to have the main dish. Then, you go down town to have vegetables. By the time you are finished it is 10 o'clock at night and you are still hungry because you have never eaten enough at one place to get really full. Some people call this fun. If that is you, good for you. This whole plan will be easier for you. But, if you are not into big and elaborate, this story illustrates that it doesn't have to be big and elaborate. I have often asked groups at my seminars to brain-storm 20 things that they might could do as a group. I ask them to think about the calendar. Start with Christmas. There is one, you could do a Christmas party, then a New Year's party.

What is next? Some people always miss this, but next is a Super Bowl party.

A lot of churches have some controversy about what to do on the Super Bowl. They normally have Sunday night services. If you ever attend one of these churches on Sunday night, you will discover that a lot of people are voting with their feet. They are voting against having church on the night of the Super Bowl. So many are voting that way, that some people have actually brought it up in the business meeting of some of these churches, "I think we should cancel our Sunday night service on the night of the Super Bowl." No matter how you spin that, it doesn't sound too spiritual. Cancel church for football? How can that be of God. So, the controversy begins.

Let me weigh in here. I think the most spiritual thing you can do on the night of the Super Bowl is cancel your Sunday night service and ask each group to have a party. If you have someone in your group that has a big screen TV, they make an ideal candidate for your Super Bowl party.

By the way, this whole strategy works a lot better if you have a big screen TV. It is likely God's will that you buy a big screen TV. It's a ministry. I think if you were really dedicated, you would buy a big screen TV. Good news is if you disagree with me at this point, you can still be used by God in the ministry of giving Friday nights to Jesus.

Let me invite you to think of 20 things you could do. Again, start with the calendar. I have filled in the first four. You are not committing to anything, just brainstorming about what you could do:

1. Christmas party
2. New Years Eve party
3. Super Bowl Party
4. Valentine's Party
5. _____
6. _____
7. _____
8. _____
9. _____
10. _____
11. _____
12. _____
13. _____
14. _____
15. _____
16. _____
17. _____

18. _____
19. _____
20. _____

Now that you have made your list, let me say that you don't actually have to have a list. Some people like that. They like lists. They like big and elaborate. They like decoration and preparation and foo-foo. It that is you, if you like foo-foo, good for you. This ministry will be easier for you. But, I want to reach out to the people who don't like big and elaborate. It doesn't have to be big and elaborate. In the case of this group, they did the same fellowship every month at the same restaurant on the same night of the month. They didn't have a list of 20; they had a list of 1.

I have known a couple of groups that did full-week vacations together every summer. How are you doing with that idea right there? How would you like to take a full week vacation with your small group? How would you like to hang with your Sunday School class 24 hours a day, for a week? For me? Not so much. That is more community that I require. But, if you are into that kind of thing, good for you. Invite every member and every prospect to every vacation every summer. I don't know how many people you will get to come, but if they do come, they will be a thoroughly assimilated member by the time the week is over.

The details

Success if often in the details. It is not in understanding the broad principles; it is in execution of the details. So, let's talk through the details.

Who to invite

Jesus said, "Don't invite only your friends." So, invite your best friends, but don't stop there. Invite people who are members of your group but don't come all that often. I have seen it happen more times than I could count that if I could get them to class, I couldn't keep them from the party.

Invite prospects. One of the best sources of prospects is visitors to your church. Most churches have plenty of visitors. The challenge is getting the visitors to stick around. One of the best ways of getting them to stick around is to invite them to your home for an evening of Diet Coke, coffee cake and card playing.

Invite friends, neighbors, and co-workers who are not walking with Christ. Truthfully, I think this is a more noble thing, but quite honestly, we concentrated on recent visitors. If you have plenty of visitors, this is an equally valid strategy. There is something to be said about going after the reachable while they are reachable. Pick the fruit when it is ripe. The most reachable people in town are the people who are visiting in your worship services.

If you don't have many visitors, I have a suggestion. Take really good care of the visitors you do have. I had a host tell me recently that the established members hardly ever invited guests, but their new-comers did. People inside your church don't know all that many people on the outside. Newcomers do. If you take really good care of your newcomers, they will tend to bring more newcomers. It is John Maxwell's law of the big Mo. Momentum is everything. It is why it is easy for growing churches to grow and it is difficult for plateaued churches to start growing. Difficult, but not impossible. One of the best ways to get started is to take really good care of your visitors. They will tend to bring their friends and you will get more visitors.

What to do

Play. Laugh. Accept them. Include the guests in everything. Continue to follow up until you sense they are thoroughly assimilated.

I had in an interesting lesson once in the ministry of hospitality. There was a period of time when we were interrupted from group life. We had visited a church a time or two, but had not gotten really plugged in. My Sunday School teacher called me one day and said, "Hey, a bunch of us are going to get together this Friday night and do a hay ride. We were wondering if you would like to come." I thought, "This is cool. I have always lived this out from the viewpoint of the provider; for the first time I will live it out from the viewpoint of the visitor.

By this point the concept of Friday night for Jesus was a well developed concept for me. I had done seminars, and the book, *You Can Double Your Class in Two Years or Less* was written, though not published. I added one chapter after this night.

I had always thought of a party just being about the party. But I learned, looking at it from the outside, that a party actually has three parties. The party itself is sandwiched between the pre-party and the post-party. This night was the perfect example, but it mirrored the way we had done parties as well.

It was announced that the party would start at 7.00. The truth is, they had no intention whatsoever of starting the party until sometime after 7.30. They intentionally started the party thirty minutes late so people could stand around in little clusters of 4 - 6 people and chat about the picky details of their lives.

Love at its best is a little bit boring

Love is boring because life is boring. Every life has a certain routine-ness to it. Every life has a certain predictability about it. A lot of people think my life is real exciting because I fly about 100,000 miles a year. I just passed a million life-time miles on American Airlines alone. And, I occasionally get to do some fun stuff. We had a down day on the road last summer and got to go parasailing. That was fun. I have gotten to attend some famous churches like Willowcreek and Saddleback and the original Calvary Chapel in Costa Mesa, California.

But, most of my life is another hotel room, another rental car, another church somewhere, and three more hours in D.F.W. airport. But when I call home to my wife, she will often ask me, "What kind of car did you rent?" And, when she asks about the boring details of my life, I feel loved. Love at its best is a little bit boring. It is living life in the details. It is sharing about the minutiae of life.

Back to our story.

Are you on the inside?

This group delayed the beginning of the party so that they could gather in little groups of 4 - 6 people and talk about the picky, boring details—the minutiae of their lives. I am convinced they did it on purpose.

I remembered my young married adult days. The ladies used to get together every month and tell the same stories about having the same babies—in all of it glorious detail. What they cut—or didn't, where they poked, drugs—or not, smells, fluids, sounds, people—details, details, details.

About the second time they got into this, the guys would mosey over to a different part of the hall.

There tend to be two different kind of guy groups. There are the manly-men guy groups. These are the guys who like to hunt and fish and camp and read Field and Stream magazine, shop at Home Depot, and throw rocks at little animals. I never really fit too well with this crowd. My idea of camping is Camp Marriot. My idea of roughing it is Motel 6. I hardly ever rough it.

But, happily, there was a group of guys I did fit with. These are not the manly men so much as these are the gizmo guys. I hesitate to mention any specific gizmos because as soon as I do, they will be passé by the time this book goes to print. They don't shop at Home Depot, they shop at Best Buy. They love to talk about how big their hard drives are, how much RAM they have and the latest technological breakthroughs. They have a phone that is also a G.P.S. and a Palm and surfs the web, sends and receives email, does Blackberry, Blue-tooth, sends and receives faxes and has an ice-cream machine on the side. They love to talk about their gizmos, gadgets and toys. They have never received a present that didn't plug in.

We find it very pleasurable clustering into these groups of 4 - 6 people and talking about the minutiae of our lives. We find it so pleasurable that all week long we look forward to the weekend and on the weekend–thank God it is Friday–we are ready to party. And, what do we do when we get to the party? We start the party thirty minutes late so we can cluster in these groups of 4 - 6 and talk about the minutiae of life.

And, it is a lot of fun. It is a wonderful way to live. . . if. If, you are on the inside. Have you ever been on the outside? I had never been on the outside until that night. That night we stood there for half an hour and no one invited us into their little cluster. You could argue that if we had been a little more assertive, we could have shouldered our way into one of those clusters and those good people probably would have let us in. Probably. But, we were going through a difficult time in life and didn't have what it takes to shoulder our way into someone else's cluster. And if we wait for the world to shoulder their way into our clusters, we will be waiting a long time. Jesus spoke of going out into the highways and byways and compelling them to come. The thought of strangers having to shoulder their way into the church speaks very badly of Christ's church.

The rest of the story

After a while, someone made an announcement that we were going to go take a hay ride to a different part of the farm and do a bon fire. The only people we had any familiarity with that night was our Sunday School teacher and his wife. They were sitting on a bail of hay on one of the trailers. We went and sat next to them. Before long, their little clusters moseyed over. When they got to the foot of the trailer, they began counting. You could see them counting on their hands. They worked out the math and discovered that there wasn't going to be enough room for us, our teachers, the guy group and the girl group on this trailer. So, they made eye contact with our teachers, then motioned for them to get up, which they did. They all walked off to a different trailer and left us sitting by ourselves.

I say all this to say: it is not enough to invite them, you have to be nice to them.

The really sad thing is, I have heard more stories than I would want to recount about people who have been treated in a similar way.

You need to come to the party with the same attitude of a pastor attending a party. I don't know if you know this about pastors, and it is not true of every pastor, but often pastors will attend a party every night of the month of December. Often a pastor will attend three parties on the night of New Years eve—one at 7:00, another at 9:00, and a third at 11:00. They don't do this because they have that much need for community. They don't do that because they have that much need for fellowship. They do it, not to be served, but to serve. They do it to connect, to get to know, to relate to. They do it because that is what pastors do.

If you are a teacher, I want to invite you to think of yourself as the pastor of your micro-church. I want you to go to the party with the same attitude as a pastor. You need to go to the party, not to connect with your friends, but to reach out to people who have no friends.

What not to do

Don't be theological

Don't get out a flip chart and go over six reasons to believe in the existence of God. We don't need a PowerPoint on common objections to the gospel and answers to each one of those objections. Just hang out, play games, enjoy Diet Coke, and be their friend. If you will be their friend, their heart will warm up to a message about, "What a friend we have in Jesus."

Don't share the gospel.

OK, if someone asks, "What must I do to be saved?" You can tell them. But, in my experience, the great need of the hour is not so much to tell about grace; the great need of the hour is to be gracious to people.

They do need to hear the words about grace. At the end of the day, you are not going to coffee-cake them into the kingdom. They are going to come into the kingdom in response to truth. Someone must speak the words of truth to them. They will not figure it out because of what nice people we are. We must share the words about grace. But, if we will be gracious to them, they tend to stick around long enough to hear the words about grace. They will come to our worship service and a pastor will tell them, or a teacher will tell them in a lesson, or someone will tell them privately. They do need to hear the words about grace, but we also need to be gracious to them.

Someone asked me the other night, "Do you intentionally bring up spiritual things?" No. But, we don't avoid the subject either.

The old school worked like this:
- We started with content delivery. We paid a visit, or talked to someone about Christ in the neighborhood or marketplace.
- If they responded positively, we talked to them about

coming to church. (When we said "church" we normally meant the worship service. I would argue that an equally valid expression of church is the small group, the Sunday School class, the micro-church. But, usually, when people say, "come to church," they mean, "attend the worship service.")

- If this goes well, then we talk to them about coming to a small group or Sunday School class.
- If this goes well, and definitely in the nice-to-have, not in the must-have category, we invite them to come to a fellowship that the group might have.

So, it is content-delivery, church, small-group, fellowship. I'd suggest in this day we are better off turning this process on its head. Start with the fellowship. I have seen it happen more times than I can count that if we get them to the fellowship, we couldn't keep them from class. Then, they will come to church. Or, maybe they will start with church, then we invite them to the fellowship, then they will come to class. The point is, we need to move the fellowship car up near the front of the train.

Don't do anything to make them feel like they are a crummy sinner and you have it all together

I will promise you, this is what outsiders have on their mind. This is a big deal to them. This is why they have stayed away from church up until now. They are afraid something will happen that will make them feel like they are a crummy sinner and you have it all together.

The more conservative you are, the bigger a problem this is. I have lived a very conservative life. I grew up in a missionary's home and a preacher's home and have chosen to walk in a very conservative lifestyle.

For example, I hardly ever watch R-Rated movies. I have seen a few, but it is rare. When the movie The Passion of the Christ came out I remember complaining to a friend about the fact that they made it an R-Rated movie. I didn't like that because I don't go to R-Rated movies. My friend pointed out that Jesus didn't die a G-Rated death. Good point.

When we have people over for dinner and a movie, it is a natural thing to bring up the topic of what kind of movies we have seen recently. Do you know what kind of movies people other than really conservative people are watching?

R-rated movies. And when that comes up, I am tempted to flop open a Bible to Romans 12.2 where it speaks of being transformed by the renewing of the mind. I want to give a lesson on how our mind is set up where it is garbage-in, garbage-out. I want to say to them that I wouldn't pollute my mind with that, and I don't think they should either. At another time, we might talk about all that, but on this night, all they will get from me is grace. "Oh really, that was a good movie? What do you know. I will make a note of that. Let me tell you what we watched the other day: Shrek. That was a great movie."

You could take my entire life-time consumption of alcohol and fit it into one shot glass. (Some of you are more conservative than me, and you don't know what a shot glass is. It is along the lines of the size of a Lord's Supper cup.) There has been a time or two I was at a wedding reception and there was a toast to the bride and the groom. I felt like it was the thing to do to participate. Maybe some of you wouldn't and I can respect that. I just want to communicate, that I am toward the right of the spectrum.

When you start reaching out to people, you will discover that some of them live different kinds of lives. I am thinking of one time we did a Red Lobster Valentines' dinner. Truthfully, drinking is not a huge part of this couple's life, but, once in a while, when they go out for a nice, white table-cloth dinner, they generally have a white wine with their meal. So, they came to this Southern Baptist Church Sunday School party at Red Lobster. What did they order? White wine. What did I do? I thought about getting a box and standing up on it and saying, "Hear ye, Hear ye! We are Baptist people and we don't drink wine," but that didn't seem quite right, so I ignored the situation altogether.

But, I knew that this could be problematic as well. I don't know how much you know about Baptists, but we, as a people, are not real freed up on the topic of drinking. In fact, this could be a deal-killing, job-losing issue for me. Seriously. If it got to be a normal practice that we had an open bar at our young married adult parties, I would lose my job. Guaranteed. Baptists can get pretty dialed up about this sort of thing.

So, what do we do? I didn't feel good about embarrassing this guy. And, ignoring it could be problematic. So, I took him out to lunch. "I don't know how much you know about Baptists, but we are not real freed up on the topic of drinking." "Uh-oh. Am I in trouble?" "No, you are not in trouble and here is the deal. If you and your wife go out to

Red Lobster, and it is your deal, you drink or not drink; it is totally up to you. If you want to have some people over to your home, what you serve or not is totally up to you. But, if this is a Calvary Baptist Church Sunday School party, if you could refrain from drinking at those events, it would really help us out. I would get to keep my job and we could rock along here just fine." He totally understood; you just have to be careful how you handle it.

A friend told me about a time he was invited to a Sunday School party. In his world, when you came to a party, the decent, couth, thing to do was to bring a bottle of wine. Nothing really special or unusual about this; it is just what you do. In Baptist circles, you bring a plate of cookies. In his circle, you brought a bottle of wine. So, he came to this Southern Baptist Church Sunday School party. He brought what he always brought, a bottle of wine. He told me, "To this day I don't know what happened to that bottle of wine." Last I knew, that man was preaching to 1200 people a week in Kentucky. I shudder to think where he might be if he met some of my Baptist friends at the door who would have made sure he understood that we are Baptist people and we don't drink wine. You just have to be careful in those moments that you don't do anything to make them feel like they are a crummy sinner.

My friend Sam told me about a time when his wife, Ruthe, was teaching a new members class. She had a 65-year old ex-sailor in her class. (It is important to the story that you understand he was an ex-sailor.) At the end of the hour, she asked for a volunteer to lead in prayer. The ex-sailor volunteered, "Lord, this has been one helluva Bible study..." You have to be careful in those moments.

Another time we had a couple reciprocate and have us into their home. They had been in our home many times, so they thought it would be nice to have us over. I will never forget the night John welcomed me into his home with this greeting, "Can I get you something to drink? We have Diet Coke, iced tea, Dr. Pepper and cold beer. Cold beer. Hmmm. That is the only time in my life I have been asked that question. I just have not run in those circles. I politely asked for a Diet Coke. I was calm on the outside, but on the inside, I was totally excited. On the inside, I was saying to myself, "Boy! We have a real live pagan on our hands!" I thought this because I know that Baptists who move to town from Alabama know that Baptist ministers don't drink cold beer in public. So, I knew we had a real live pagan on our hands. Now, as it turns out, he was not a pagan after all, he was a Presbyterian. They are a little more freed up on this topic. You know that old saying about Presbyterians, "Where two or three are gathered together, there is also a fifth."

We have to be careful in that moment not to do anything to make them feel like they are a crummy sinner and you have it all together.

There are a wide variety of ways you can give Friday nights to Jesus. Make yourself some notes. What are some ways this could work for you?

_____
_____
_____
_____
_____
_____
_____

The Epidemic of Loneliness

Vietnam Veteran William Broyles wrote:
"A part of me loved war."

"Now, please understand, I am a peaceful man, fond of children and animals. And, I believe that war should have no place in the affairs of men. But, the comradeship our platoon experienced in that war provides a moving and enduring memory in me. A comrade in war is someone you can trust with anything, because you regularly trust him with your life. In war, individual possessions and advantage count for nothing. The group, the unit, the platoon is everything." Loved war? The Vietnam war? This was the war we hated. This was the war we protested. This was the war we burned our draft cards and fled to Canada over.

The other day at D.F.W. airport they made the boarding announcement a different way. There was a group of soldiers home from Iraq for a short period of time. When they announced that the soldiers would be boarding first, the boarding area burst into spontaneous applause. The post 9/11 era is an era of national pride and patriotism. We applaud our soldiers. Not so the Vietnam era. But this soldier said, "There was a part of me that loved war." How could he say such a thing?

He could say such a thing because sociologists looking at the culture have said, "There is an epidemic of loneliness in the culture."

Perhaps the most definitive work on this topic was written by Robert Putnam. It is not your garden variety theoretician musing about his own experience. Rather, this is a carefully researched, well documented book based on extensive research. They got a large government grant, put together a research team and over several years analyzed every available bit of data. This is what they found.
During the first two-thirds of the last century Americans took a more and more active role in the social and political life of their communities—in churches and card tables and dinner tables.
Year by year we gave more generously to charity, we pitched in more often on community projects, and we behaved in an increasingly trustworthy way toward one another.
Then, mysteriously and more or less simultaneously, we began to do all these things less often.

To prove his point, Putnam includes forty graphs in the back of the book. Here are a few of them.

Here is participation in associations over the past 100 years:

Figure 8. Average Membership Rate in Thirty-two National Chapter-Based Associations, 1900-1997

You can see the gradual trend upward through most of the last century. There is a dip during the years of the great depression, then the trend moves right back up, then levels off in the decade of the 60s, and has been declining ever since.

There is a similar pattern in membership in unions.

Figure 14: Union Membership in the United States, 1900–1998

The PTA shows an especially dramatic trend line:

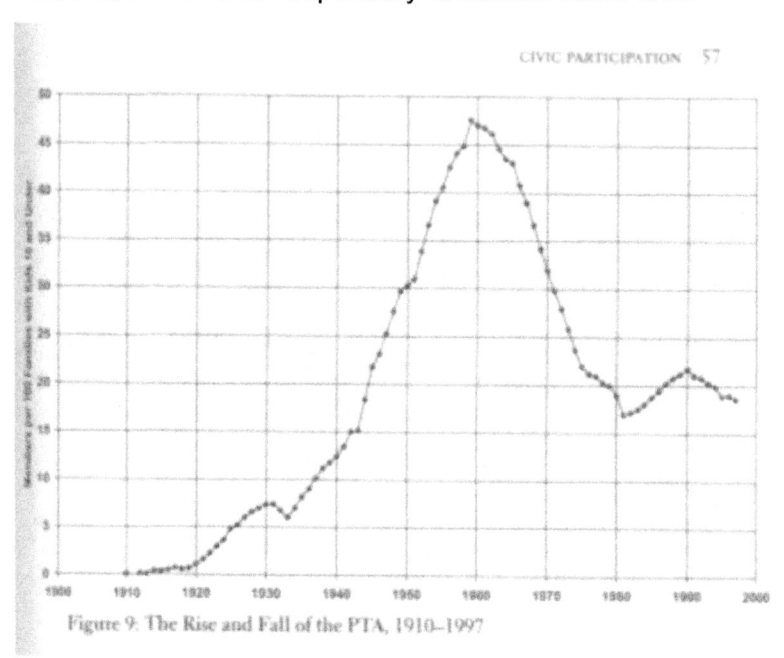

Figure 9: The Rise and Fall of the PTA, 1910–1997

These next several graphs zoom in on the last half of the last century. The vertical lines still represent decades; notice there are not as many of them. This one is participation in organizations of various kinds:

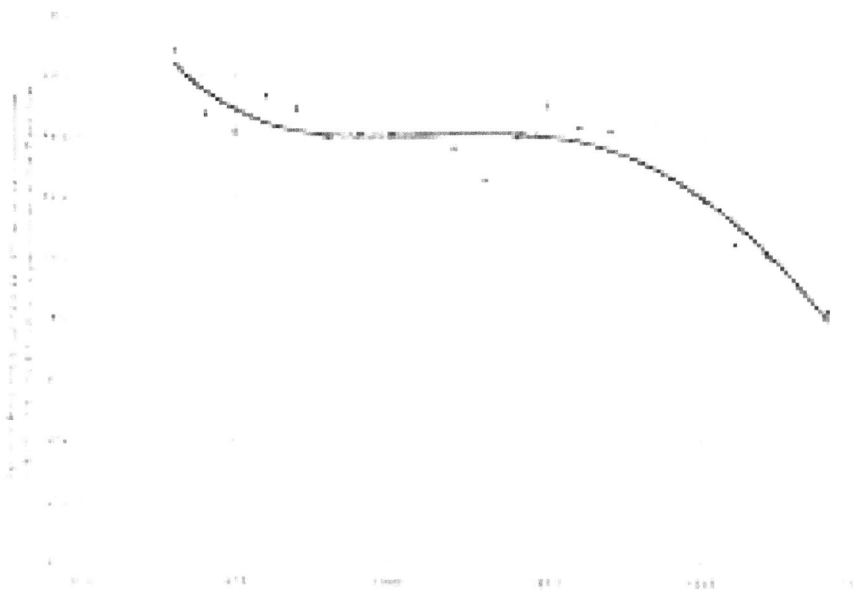

Informal socializing shows a similar pattern:

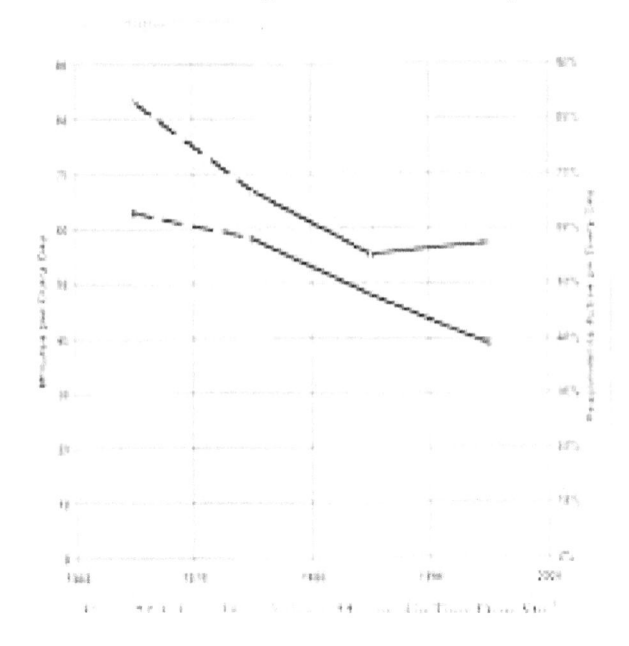

Clubs have been on the decline:

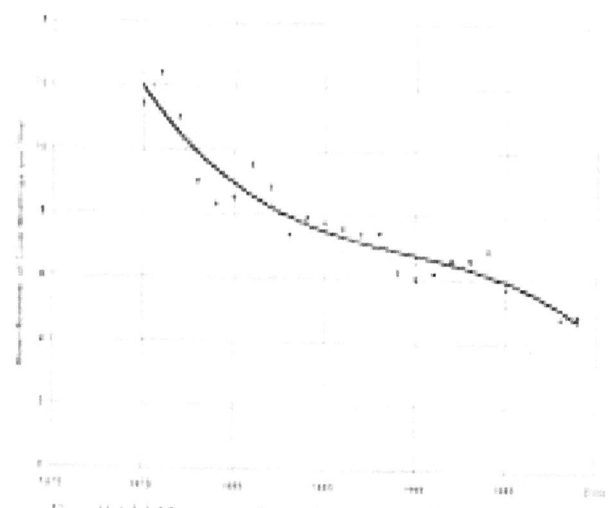

People are not playing cards with their friends as often as they used to:

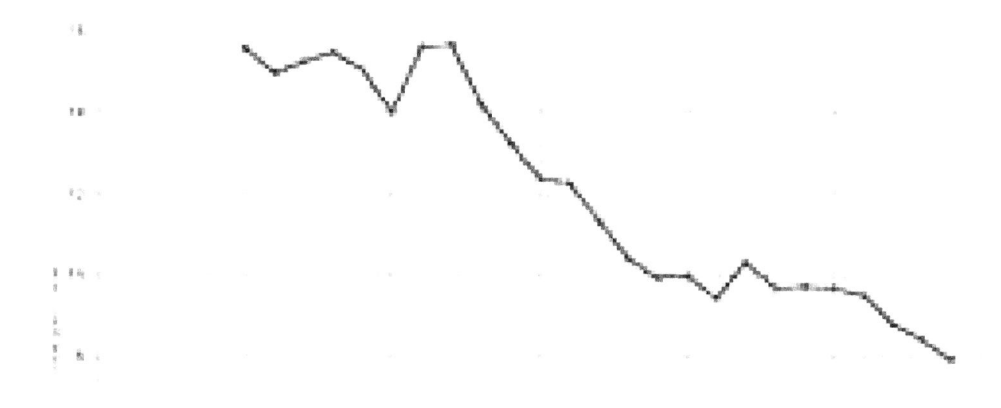

The book gets its title from this last graph. The name of the book is *Bowling Alone*. The top line represents how often men joined bowling leagues over the last century. The lower line represents how often women joined bowling leagues. I had a bowling alley owner come up to me after a conference and affirm to me the reality of this graph. He said he had seen it lived out before his eyes. For him, it was not theory or academia. For him, it was business; it was life.

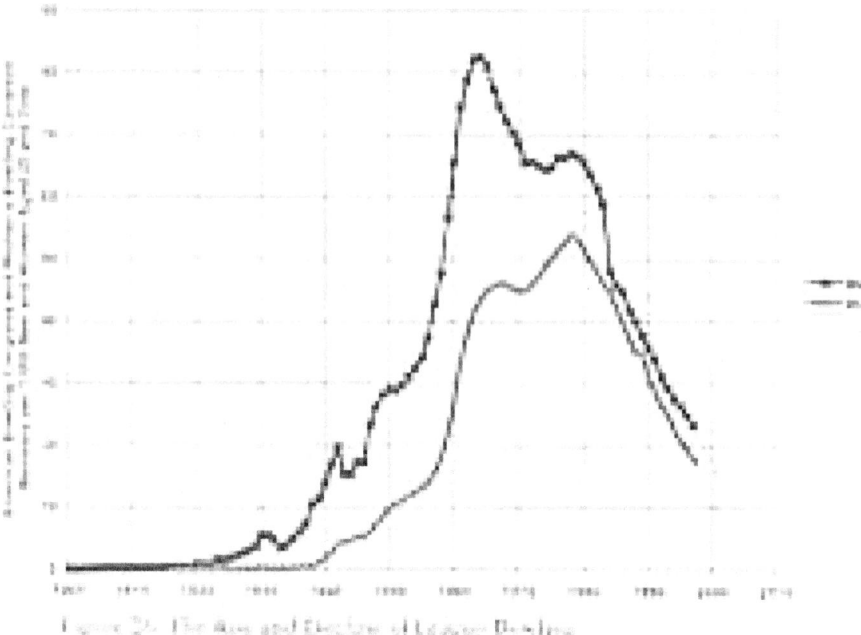

Figure 25. The Rise and Decline of League Bowling

Do you believe it?

I have presented this material enough to know the reaction from many.

Some are skeptical. They tend to doubt the data. Their attitude is, "I don't care how many graphs you show me. I don't care how much money they spend on this research. I don't care how many degrees this professor has, I just don't believe it." Some feel this way because it is not a reflection of the way leaders in the church tend to live. We are constantly going and doing and seeing and sipping coffee with and eating with and talking on the phone to.

Here is what I want to invite you to see: the world lives a very different life than you do. There is an epidemic of loneliness in the culture. They don't have friends any more. Maybe that is why they like watching Friends on TV. They like to imagine a place like Cheers, where everybody knows your name, or, at least, where somebody knows your name.

Have you ever been lonely?

Have you ever been lonely? I mean, really lonely? I have lived most of my life on the inside, but there has been a time or two when we were interrupted from group life. Due to a move, or other circumstances, we were not plugged into group life.

I will never forget the night my father-in-law passed away. I am a heavy sleeper, so my wife took the call. She shook my feet and awakened me, saying two words that shocked me out of my groggy slumber, "Daddy died."

I hugged her and held her and we talked a bit. Then, I started thinking logistics. I remembered that her van was in the shop. My car had just gotten out of the shop. They had done some work on the radiator. Apparently, one of the hoses was installed incorrectly and rubbed up against one of the fan belts. When I pulled into the driveway, water was spewing like a fire hydrant. At the time, I thought, "Not to worry. I will let it cool off, fill it up with water and drive it back down to the shop. It will easily make it back to the shop." I also knew it was not in any shape to take a road trip that night.

I remember sitting on my bed and dropping my face in my hands and thinking, "I can't think of a single person I know well enough to call in the middle of the night and ask to borrow a car." Do you have any idea what that feels like? Have you ever been really lonely?

I have lived most of my life within the warmth of a loving Christian community. But this night, I tasted a strong dose of the pain of loneliness. It is how much of the world lives most of the time. It is awful.

The medical consequences of loneliness

The *Bowling Alone* project studied not only what has been going on–the lack of "social capital," as Putnam calls it, but also the result of this lack of social capital. The results are alarming.

One study was based in Alameda county, California. For 9 years researchers followed 7,000 people to discern their lifestyle habits—how often they attend groups, when they go to meetings, any clubs they participate in and so forth. In addition, they studied health rates, incidence of death and the like. Here is what they discovered. People who are not in a group are twice as likely to die in the next year as those who are in a group. Now, there is a selling point for your small group ministry! You might want to mention that to people. "Join one of our groups and cut in half your chances of dying in the next year. Joining a group has roughly the same health benefit as quitting smoking or joining the gym.

Here is another salient quote: "People who have strong social connections, but poor health habits (eating, exercise, smoking, etc.) are just as healthy as those with good health habits but weak social connections." There are a lot of adjectives in that sentence, so let me paraphrase this in the words of John Ortberg: "Better to eat Twinkies with friends than broccoli alone."

This one is my favorite. They did a study where they injected 270 people with a virus that causes the common cold. This was written up in the journal of the American Medical

Association. The difference between the two groups was not subtle. There was a difference of a factor of about 4:1. Those with strong social connections didn't get as sick (by a factor of about 4:1), when they did get sick, they didn't stay sick as long (by a factor of about 4:1), and they produced less mucus than the less connected group. Somebody measured.

Again, let me paraphrase Ortberg here: "It goes to show—unfriendly people really are snottier than friendly people." We have the biological data to prove it.

This epidemic of loneliness creates a kind of opportunity for us. Because of the epidemic of loneliness, there is an incredible ministry opportunity for us.

I grew up as a missionaries' kid in the Philippines. One of the laws of missions is, "Use the felt needs of the culture to reach the culture." In other words, if we find a culture that is hungry for physical bread, we find they are far more likely to listen to a message about the Bread of Life if we attend first to their need for physical bread. In a similar way, if we will be a friend to people, their heart starts to warm up to a message about "What a friend we have in Jesus." If we will love them, their heart starts to warm up to a message about a God who loves them.

There may have been a day when evangelism by content delivery was enough. We simply delivered the message, the information, about a God who loves them and invited them to accept the message. In a culture where there is an epidemic of loneliness, we need to do more. We need to represent God to them in terms of actually loving them. It is not enough to talk about a God that loves them. We must love them.

Seen graphically, it looks like this.

Sharing Christ

leads to

invite to church

leads to

invite to Sunday School or small group

leads to

invite to a Sunday School or small group party.

The last one–invite to Sunday School or small group party–is definitely in the nice-to-do, not the must-do category.

I would suggest, because of the epidemic of loneliness in our culture, we are better off turning the whole thing on its head. Start with the party.

Invite to a party

leads to

coming to class and church

leads to

hearing the gospel message presented

leads to

becoming a Christian

There is an epidemic of loneliness in the culture. Because of that we need to love, not merely talk about love. If we love them, their heart will warm up to a message about a God who loves them. If we will be their friend, their heart will warm up to a message about what a friend they can have in Jesus.

The Joy of Total Dedication

It is commonly asserted that the price of following Christ is, well, there is no price. It is a free gift. It is absolutely a free gift and any other perspective calls into question the whole concept of grace.

There is some truth in this, for the Bible says, "For the wages of sin is death, but the free gift of God is eternal life through Christ Jesus our Lord." Romans 6:23 (NLT) Technically speaking the word "free" does not appear in the Greek, only the word charisma, or gift. The NIV bears this out: "For the wages of sin is death, but the gift of God is eternal life in Christ Jesus our Lord." Romans 6:23 (NIV) Still, a gift is, by definition free. If it is earned then it is a wage, which is the whole point of the comparison in this verse. That is one, valid, perspective. But, it is not the only perspective, because it is not the only thing the Bible says about the topic.

In another place, Jesus says, "In the same way, any of you who does not give up everything he has cannot be my disciple." Luke 14:33 (NIV)

And, this is not the only time this topic comes up. Jesus disciples clearly did this, they "left everything and followed him." Luke 5:11 (NIV)

Jesus used even stronger language in Luke 14.26, "If anyone comes to me and does not hate his father and mother, his wife and children, his brothers and sisters--yes, even his own life--he cannot be my disciple." Now, surely this is a bit of a hyperbole to make his point. He is not saying that we must literally hate our family. He is saying that our devotion to Christ is so intense that any other devotion is hatred by comparison. There is a cost to following Christ.

Paul echoed this teaching in Philippians 3:7 - 8, "But whatever was to my profit I now consider loss for the sake of Christ. What is more, I consider everything a loss compared to the surpassing greatness of knowing Christ Jesus my Lord, for whose sake I have lost all things. I consider them rubbish, that I may gain Christ" Philip. 3:7-8 (NIV)

Paul had found the pearl of great price, the treasure hidden in the field. Like the man in Jesus' story, he gladly gave up everything to have it. Notice that price the men in Jesus story pay to get the treasure and the pearl: "The kingdom of heaven is like treasure hidden in a field. When a man found it, he hid it again, and then in his joy went and sold all he had and bought that field. Again, the kingdom of heaven is like a merchant looking for fine pearls. When he found one of great value, he went away and sold everything he had and bought it". Matthew 13:44-46 (NIV)

What did the field cost? Was it free? No, in fact, it was extremely expensive. (Although, anyone has enough to have it. He must give up all he has, but it is enough.) What did the pearl cost, was it free? No, it cost everything as well.

Reconciling costly grace and free grace

How do we reconcile the concept that grace is free, yet also very costly—so costly we must give up everything to have it? Perhaps the best way is the way that Jesus usually taught, through a story.

Imagine a beggarly orphan child living on the street. He has nothing but rags—the clothes on his back and an old, tattered, dirty, smelly blanket.

The richest man in the world has pity on this child and decides to do something. He decides to take him in as his own child. He will write him in as the sole heir to the rich man's fortune. The boy will have access to the finest education, the funnest toys, the most exciting vacations–the best of everything.

But, it is not merely material wealth the richest man in the world wants to give this boy. He wants to be his father. He wants to give him himself. He plans to play with him and talk with him and take him places and treat him as his own son.

"What will it cost me?" the boy thinks out loud. "Nothing." the richest man in the word responds, "Nothing at all. I gladly give you all this."

As he makes his way into the house, the richest man in the world notices he is still carrying his old, tattered, smelly blanket. "Oh, you won't be needing this, son. Discard it outside." "Discard it outside? I could never do that. I have had this blanket with me my whole life. It has been my sole possession for as long as I can remember. I can't get rid of that." "Oh, son, you don't understand, I will give you your pick of the finest blankets made. We will spend a whole day shopping together. You can buy a dozen blankets if you want to and try them out and see which one you like. If you can't decide among them, keep them all. You don't need that old, tattered, smelly blanket." "I know it is silly, sir, but I can't part with this blanket. Did you see the movie Cast Away? This is my "Wilson". I can't part with it."

"Son, I am prepared to take you in as my own son, to give you my heart, as well as giving you access to all my possessions. I will leave you everything I have. You will be the richest man in all the world. But, you must give up that blanket."

Now, two things are true. It will cost the boy everything if he wants to come into the mansion. Second, he has nothing of any real value, and it is accurate to say that the richest man in the world is giving the boy a gift–an incredible gift. Both are true. It costs him everything and it is free.

God would fill our hands with spiritual gold, but we must drop the dirt from our hands. We can't have the gold if we don't.

Israel had to leave Egypt to enter the promised land.

Bait and switch?

The subject of Lordship comes up in Christian teaching, but it doesn't normally come up under the topic of salvation. Sometimes, the whole Lordship issue is seen as a kind of advanced discipleship. Sometimes, it is presented as an optional path for super-Christians. If you want to be a normal Christian, just receive the free gift, if you want to be a super-Christian, you can opt in to the Lordship option.

Setting aside the theological ramifications of all of this, I can't help but think it could feel like a bit of a bait and switch to many. We present the gospel of the free gift, only to tell them later that what is really involved is lordship and total commitment. Jesus seemed to deal with the Lordship issue right up front.

Good news or bad news?

I used to see this issue of Lordship as the bad news, the hidden fine print of the Christian faith. I have found myself a little embarrassed when talking to outsiders about Christ. I occasionally used the lordship truth to beat up on complacent church members. I no longer see it that way. I no longer see it as the hidden fine print of the Christian life, but the best part of all, the part that makes Christian living all that.

I think a lot of believers see the Christian faith this way. It is kind of a faith of good news and bad news.

The good news is, God loves you and has a wonderful plan for your life. The bad news is, the wonderful plan includes more than a small amount of suffering.

The good news is, God would offer you eternal life as a free gift. The bad news is, oh, by the way, it actually is very costly–it costs you everything.

The good news is God is a God of love and compassion and mercy and grace. The bad news is, He is also a God of justice and wrath.

We justify the preaching of a good news and bad news gospel because it is not *all* bad news. It is not like those pulpit-pounding, hang-them-over-hell, scream and stomp and shout and spit and "you are sinning and you need to quit" crowd. "We preach a balanced gospel," we like to console ourselves.

A little bit of grace to make you feel loved; a little bit of condemnation to make you behave. That is *not* the gospel of the New Testament. "There is therefore now no condemnation." (Romans 8.1) Not a little; NO condemnation. It is all about good news, good news and more good news.

There are three problems with this gospel of good news and bad news. **First, you will never get all that wholehearted about living it.** We are irrevocably hard-wired to pursue what we perceive to be in our best interest. We can't avoid the programing. We can't get past it. In the long run, we will do what we perceive to be in our best interest. You will never really embrace a gospel you perceive to be a gospel of good news and bad news.

Second, you will never get all that excited about telling others about it. I think many Christians fail to talk about their faith because it is just not that interesting to them. It is a gospel of good news and bad news, and only mildly interesting. They are reasonably pleased with the Christian faith. But, reasonably pleased customers don't tell their friends. It takes ecstatic customers to pull off a movement.

Churches are looking today for better methods of growing our churches. What we need to be looking for is a different gospel. We need to abandon the gospel of good news and bad news. We need to embrace the gospel of good news, good news and more good news.

There is a third reason we need to abandon the gospel of good news and bad news. It isn't true. You don't find it anywhere in the Bible. The gospel of the Bible is the gospel of good news, good news and more good news.

The gospel of good news, good news, and more good news.

There have been a number of biblical truths that I learned outside of the Bible, only to discover later that they were in the Book all along. The Friday Nights for Jesus concept was that. I discovered it when we had some people over for Diet Coke, coffee cake and card playing and saw them place their faith in Christ and join our church. It wasn't until later that I discovered the verse that says, "Get into the habit of inviting guests home for dinner." (Romans 12.13, NLT) The gospel of good news, good news and more good news was discovered in a similar way. I learned it outside of the Bible, only to discover that it had been in the Book the whole time.

I have been a life-long student of happiness. Even as a child I was consciously aware of the goal to live a happy life. This goal was crystalized when I read John Piper's book, *Desiring God.* This is arguably the best book I have ever read. Piper paraphrases the Westminster Shorter Catechism this way, "What is the chief end of man? The chief end of man is to glorify God by enjoying Him forever." Here is a great line:

"God is most glorified in us when we are most satisfied in Him." Piper quotes verses like Philippians 4.4, "Rejoice in the Lord always," and Psalm 37.4, "Delight yourself in the Lord." Piper found a quote by C.S. Lewis that I was unaware of, "It is a Christian duty, as you know, to be as happy as you can be." Indeed.

It occurred to me as I read this that this is the problem in many churches. It is not that we need better programs or fresh ideas or new plans. The problem is, we are about half-bored with this whole deal called Christianity. Show me a people who are thoroughly obedient to the command of God to, "Rejoice in the Lord always" and I will show you a people who are turning our world upside down. Reading Piper focused my quest to pursue joy.

Flow

I read a number of books on joy, some Christian, some secular, to learn whatever I could on this important topic. One of the best was Martin Seligman's classic, *Authentic Happiness.* Seligman's work has been featured on the cover of New York Times, Time, Newsweek, U.S. News and World Report, the Reader's Digest, Redbook, Parents, Fortune, Family Circle, and many other popular magazines. His 20 books have been translated into 16 languages and have been best sellers in America and abroad. He was elected as the president of the American Psychological Association by the largest vote in modern history.

Most psychologists have studied psychological illness—schizophrenia, depression and so forth. Seligman has concentrated on psychological health—what makes for optimum psychological functioning. *Authentic Happiness* represents the culmination of a life of work along these lines.

A core insight that Seligman provided was related to another work, Mihaly Csikszentmihalyi's *Flow*. Csikszentmihalyi describes flow as the optimal human condition. It is that moment when time stands still, when you want to live in that moment.

I have called this the 3:14 state, based on Paul's words in Philippians 3:14. "I press on toward the goal to win the prize for which God has called me heavenward in Christ Jesus." That pressing on describes the state of flow. Csikszentmihalyi describes it in some other ways.

He describes a dancer who says, "Your concentration is very complete. Your mind isn't wandering, you are not thinking of something else; you are totally involved in what you are doing. . . Your energy is flowing very smoothly. You feel relaxed, comfortable, and energetic." That is the 3:14 state.

A rock climber: "You are so involved in what you are doing [that] you aren't thinking of yourself as separate from the immediate activity. . . You don't see yourself as separate from what you are doing." That is the 3:14 state.

A mother speaks of her daughter: "Her reading is the one thing that she's really into, and we read together. She reads to me, and I read to her, and that's a time when I sort of lose touch with the rest of the world, I'm totally absorbed in what I'm doing." That is the 3:14 state.

A chess player: ". . . the concentration is like breathing, you are never aware of it. The roof could fall in, and, if it missed you, you would be unaware of it." That is the 3:14 state.

Vince Lombardi described this state when he said, "I firmly believe that any man's finest hour—this greatest fulfillment to all he holds dear—is that moment when he has worked his heart out in a good cause and lies exhausted on the field of battle— victorious."

Jesus described this state in this passage, "'My food,' said Jesus, 'is to do the will of him who sent me and to finish his work.'" John 4:34 (NIV) The context of this verse is the story of the woman at the well. The disciples come out and ask Jesus if he is hungry. "Don't you want to eat something? You should get something to eat. You are surely hungry." Jesus is saying he is so distracted by this conversation with this woman that he forgot all about eating. He was in a state of flow.

Conditions of *Flow*

What are the conditions that make this state possible?

There must be a **goal**. Flow has a certain future orientation to it. Paul said, "I press on toward the goal," and for flow to work, there must be a goal.

Brian Tracy said, "Success is all about goal setting, the rest is just commentary." Success is all about the relentless pursuit of a worthwhile goal. It is not so much about achieving a goal. It is not so much about arriving. It is about embracing the goal of seeking what we do not have.

In Christian living, we are always pursuing flying goals. We are pursuing perfection. The goal is always out there. That for which Christ laid hold of us is always just beyond our grasp.

The goal needs to be **barely achievable**. It needs to be just out of reach. It needs to be a challenge. John Ortberg poses the question, "Think about a time when God asked someone to do something and then followed it up with, 'And I have good news. This is not going to be hard at all. It is going to be a walk in the park. It is going to be a piece of cake.' God never said that." As Blackaby says, when God calls us to something, it is always a God-sized task. Bonhoeffer said it more strongly: When Jesus calls a man, he bids him come and die.

Flow requires **feedback**. Feedback is the breakfast of champions. One of the roles of leadership is to put people in a feedback loop so they know how they are doing. People are motivated as they see the score on the board. If the score is close, it adds to the flow experience.

Kenneth Blanchard, in *One Minute Manager* invites us to imagine a group of guys bowling. Instead of seeing the pins crash and fall, the pins are hidden behind a curtain. They hear the crash, but they don't see the pins fall. The pins are hidden behind the curtain. What does that do to motivation? Motivation requires feedback.

Flow requires **competence**. We have to be reasonably good at the task for the flow experience to kick in. This is what spiritual gifts do for us. They are a Divine enablement to do the things God has called us to do.

There is a feeling in flow that **this is what you were born to do.** I am blessed to feel this way a good part of the time. I spend a good deal of my life in writing and speaking—two things that, for me, create this flow experience. I am sure that these two activities would not create flow at all for someone else, but for me, there is a feeling that this is what I was born to do.

Churchill said, "There comes a special moment in everyone's life, a moment for which that person was born. That special opportunity, when he seizes it, will fulfill his mission—a mission for which he is uniquely qualified. In that moment, he finds greatness. It is his finest hour."

The last requirement for the flow experience is **total commitment**. You cannot experience flow while flipping channels playing couch potato. You have to be committed, totally committed. The rock climber is totally committed to scaling the wall. The dancer is not thinking about what she will eat for supper. The chess player is fully engaged in planning the next several moves. There is no flow for the half-hearted. You must be totally committed.

This is what Jesus called us to–total commitment. He didn't do it to punish us, He did it to give us the highest state of human functioning–flow.

This needs to move up, way up

The most insightful question I have ever been asked in response to my teaching was asked by a farmer in Littlefield, Texas. We did a Q and A at the end of the seminar, and here is what this man asked. "I have not doubt that this will work. I have seen it work and do not question at all whether it will work."

(I might say, parenthetically, that I hear this a lot. Last night after a seminar in Mississippi, someone said to me, "We started a paper class once–no real people, just names on a piece of paper. A year later we had fifty. We did it exactly as you described. She smiled as she told the story. I felt like the memory of that year was a fond memory for her. Two weeks ago in Geogia a man said to me, "Six months ago we started a class of college students. Today we have 18 attending. We did it exactly as you described." Recently I have been asking for a show of hands if people have seen this work, somewhere, sometime in their lives. Tonight was typical. Roughly two-thirds of the hands went up. People have seen this happen. They just are not doing it intentionally, systematically, and consistently. Success in almost any arena is to figure out what works, then do it systematically and consistently. What I teach is to make intentional the things we are doing accidentally. At any rate, back to the story.)

This man says, "I know this will work. I have seen it work. Here is my problem. I come to church on Sunday morning both for Sunday School and church. I come Sunday night. We have discipleship and a worship service. I come to both. We have visitation on Monday night. I try to attend. On Wednesday night we have a meal, prayer meeting and choir practice. I am involved in all three. I am a deacon, and we have meetings once a month. I am on a couple of committees that meet about as often. I have no doubt that this stuff would work, if I would work it. To be perfectly honest, I don't think I will work it. And, not because I am lazy and am spending every evening flipping channels. I am not. I am giving myself to some good things. It is just that my schedule is full. I feel I need to spend some time with my family. What advice do you have for me?"

I stood before a hundred or so curious faces. What would I tell him? What would you tell him?

You might disagree with what I told him, and I can respect that, but here is what I said. "I think you are going to have to move this up, and I want to say, 'way up' in your priority structure. In fact, if I were your pastor, I would say this to you, 'I would ask you to make giving Friday night to Jesus your second church priority. Not thinking about your global priorities of life, just your church priorities, make this #2. Your first church priority is to come on Sunday morning to worship and Sunday School. The second is to give Friday nights to Jesus. If you want to, stay home on Sunday night, stay home on Wednesday nights, get off the deacon board, quit coming to visitation and make giving Friday nights to Jesus your priority. Now, clearly you have some more time to give and we would love to have you, so perhaps you want to add back in Sunday night or Wednesday night. Add them back in whatever priority order makes sense to you. But, keep Friday nights for Jesus #2."

You may disagree with what I said to this man, and I can respect that. Here is my point. If giving Friday nights to Jesus is your fifth, sixth or seventh priority, behind Sunday morning, Sunday night, Wednesday night, choir, prayer meeting, discipleship, deacons, visitation, and then, if we have more time to give, we will do the Friday night thing—let's face it, you may as well make an open decision to never do this stuff. It won't happen. Not if it is that far down in the priority list.

Whenever we think about doing anything we have to also think about what we are not going to do. If you decide to give Friday nights to Jesus, will it come out of your church time, or your family time, or some other time?

Do you know what keeps some people from being more effective for God? Church. Church keeps some people from being more effective for God. We are so busy with church activities that we don't have time to give Friday nights to Jesus. To do so would be to violate the priority of the family.

Rick Warren has done a great service to the church by reminding us of the importance of balancing the five purposes of the church. Sunday morning addresses at least three purposes: worship, teaching/discipleship, and fellowship. It just makes sense to me that the next time slots we give have to do with evangelism and ministry.

The Bible says, "Get in the habit of inviting guests home for dinner." For it to be a habit, it has to be a priority. A high priority.

But, you will have to sort this out for yourself. I recommend you take a long walk with God and talk about this matter. If you don't end up the same place I am, that is fine; we don't all have to agree on everything. But, if we don't move this up–way up–in the priority structure, it won't be done.

The example of Jesus

The Bible says about Jesus that He "laid down his life for the sheep." (John 10:15) Notice two things about this phrase.

First, Jesus *laid down his life*. He didn't just help out. There is a difference between helping out and laying down your life. Jesus laid down his life.

Church people are good at helping out, and we appreciate the help. But, that is not what we are called to do. We are not called to help out. We are called to lay down our lives. There is a huge difference.

The difference between laying down your life and helping out can be illustrated by a scene from the movie John Q. In this movie, Denzel Washington plays the role of a hard-working, middle class, all-around good guy. Due to an economic down-turn, his job is cut to part time. Due to company policy, his insurance is cut. Part-time employees don't receive insurance benefits. His son has a heart condition and needs to be put on the list for a heart transplant. The hospital refuses to put him on the list because there is no insurance.

He pursues numerous options. He tries to work with the insurance company. He does a fund-raising drive and raises a considerable amount of money, but it is not enough, not nearly enough. Denzel's son is dying. The clock is ticking. Time is running out.

Denzel Washington's character does an unthinkable thing for this good, hard-working, middle-class guy. He holds up the emergency room of the hospital at gun point with the demand that they put his son on the list for a heart transplant. I found myself really torn as I watched the movie. On the one hand, I thought, "How could he hold the emergency room up at gun point? He seems like such a nice guy?" But, on the other hand, I thought, "If that were my kid who was dying, I might do something unthinkable to save him."

There is one moment in this emergency room drama that I'd like to draw your attention to. Two of the hostages are talking. One is the hospital guard. Another hostage says to the guard, "Why don't you do something? You are the guard. You are supposed to protect us from this kind of thing happening. Do something!"

The guard responds, "Not me. Not for $10 an hour." The guard was willing to help out; he was not willing to lay down his life."

Late in the movie Denzel's character shows that he is willing to do more than just help out. He threatens to take his own life and demands that a doctor take out his heart out of his dead body and transplant it into his son. He was willing to do more than help out. He was willing to lay down his life.

Of course, this is Hollywood, and this is Denzel Washington, so he doesn't actually have to kill himself to save his son. It all works out in typical Hollywood fashion. But, in Jesus' story, it wasn't all so pretty.

Jesus didn't just help out; he laid down his life. And, he laid down his life for sheep, the text says. Laying down your life for God, for a cause, for an ideology or a kingdom is easy. What is difficult is laying down your life for people, for sheep. As Lynn Anderson put it, sometimes, "They smell like sheep."

As someone in Oklahoma said it to me, "People in Oklahoma are kind of hard to love." Indeed.

Sometimes we say we want to reach people who are far from God, but what we mean is, we want to reach nice people. We want to reach funny people, clever people, well-dressed people, responsible people who can serve in our Sunday School and sing in our music program. God called us to reach all kinds of people and sometimes, they are kind of hard to love.

You might think that as you go to reach out to lonely people, that they will drink up your love like the desert drinks up the rain. Not true. Oh, sometimes they will. Sometimes they will be warm and receptive and will actually reciprocate your love. But, sometimes they won't. Some lonely people are lonely for a reason. They don't have good people skills. They are not funny or clever or interesting. They are rude and boring and crass and kind of hard to love.

And Jesus didn't just ask us to help out with them, he asked us to lay down our lives for them. He not only modeled it, he asked us to do the same: "This is how we know what love is: Jesus Christ laid down his life for us. And we ought to lay down our lives for our brothers." 1 John 3:16 (NIV)

It is not a punishment; it will produce the highest joy imaginable. Some of the happiest people on the planet are group leaders who are successfully changing people's lives through the ministry of hospitality. But, to get treasure, you have to sell everything; you must lay down your life.

Someone asked me once, "What is the most difficult thing you have to communicate?" By far and away the most difficult thing I have to communicate is the idea of getting people to get serious about having fun. Because this is a party-driven strategy, people tend to not take it seriously. We get serious about dedication and sacrifice, and those kind of serious issues. I want to ask you to get serious about having fun, having fun with the right people, and loving those who are far from God. I want to ask you to get serious about loving people in common, ordinary, pedestrian ways like having them into your home, feeding them your coffee cake, and playing games with them. You don't have to pay off their mortgage, or buy them a big-screen T.V. You just need to create an environment where you can talk to them about what is going on in their lives.

I want to invite you to lay down your life for the cause of loving people in common, ordinary, pedestrian ways like having them in your home and feeding them your coffee cake. Love at its best is like that. It is simple. It is boring. But, it is costly. All good ideas degenerate into work. Somebody has to buy the Diet Coke. Someone has to clean up the bathroom. It will cost you. And I want to ask you to lay down your life for it. And, it is not a burden. It is a joy. It will lead to some of the most joyous times in your life, and lead you to enjoy the flow experience of following God with all of your heart.

Flow never comes to the half-hearted. Lay down your life.

A Heart for People Far From God

What do you think about when you have nothing else to think about?

I probably think about this more than most because I live a traveling lifestyle, and in a traveling lifestyle, there is constantly down time where there is waiting and waiting and waiting. We wait to check in. We wait to board the plane. We wait after the plane is boarded. We wait when the plane lands. We wait to get our luggage. In times of waiting, where does your mind naturally drift?

It is an important question because the Bible says, "For as he thinketh in his heart, so is he." Proverbs 23:7 (KJV)

What we think about in those idle moments is a statement of who we are.

I know some people who live a traveling lifestyle, when they think about some down time, their mind drifts toward a national park or a professional ball game or a concert. When I have some down-time, my mind tends to drift in the direction of church. I think, "Is there a famous church I could attend around here somewhere?"

I have been to the original Calvary Chapel in Costa Mesa, California, birthplace of the Jesus movement of the 70s. I have been to Saddleback, birthplace of purpose. I have visited Fellowship Church in Dallas, First Baptist Atlanta, and First Baptist, Jacksonville, Florida. A couple of years ago I was in the City for the men's final of the U.S. Open Tennis Tournament in Flushing Meadows, New York. (Just happened to work out my schedule to be there on that day.) Since the tournament is Sunday afternoon, I had Sunday morning off, so I decided to visit the Brooklyn Tabernacle. WOW. What a church.

Among other things, it just did my heart good to see hundreds of people lined up outside of church for an hour or so on Sunday morning. Just like they do at your church, right? I stood in line next to a gal and began talking to her. She asked me about my day, and I asked her about hers. She said she was going to go to all three services at Brooklyn. Now, at Brooklyn the services are all alike, and they are about 2 hours long. So, I asked her, "Why are you going to go to all three services at Brooklyn?"

"What else do I have to do today but hang out at God's house all day long?"

I hate to admit this, but my immediate reaction was, "Well, the Men's final of the U.S. Open Tournament is on for one thing."

I was in Milwaukee a couple of years ago. I spoke on Friday night, Saturday morning, had Saturday night off, and spoke again on Sunday morning. I got to thinking, "How far are we from Willowcreek?" As it turns out, it was just about an hour, so we went down to Willowcreek for their Saturday night service. They had just completed their Small Group Conference and John Ortberg, then one of their preaching pastors, has spoken on the topic, "Huts of Refuge." The title didn't particularly get my attention, but I am a big fan of Ortberg, so I bought the C.D. It rocked my world. I listened to it over and over and over again. I listened so many times that, just to keep it interesting, I even listened to it in random order once, just for variety.

About a year ago, I felt like the Holy Spirit was whispering to me, "I want you to work up your own version of this talk." and I have been presenting my version as my keynote address ever since.

I can't blame everything I am going to say in this chapter on John Ortberg, but I do want to give a little credit where credit is due. God used John Ortberg to rock my world and this chapter is the echo of that experience.

John started the talk with this question, "What do you think about when you have nothing else to think about?"

You think about certain stereotypes—a businessman is constantly thinking income and expense. You go to lunch with a coach and he is constantly scribbling Xs and Os on the back of a napkin. Think about a young mom. Perhaps she has a 6-month old baby and grandma comes to her and says, "Why don't you let us watch little Johnny for the weekend?" You can send her to Orlando or Las Vegas or New York City and follow her around and no matter how distracted she is and no matter how well taken care of that baby is, you will find that she is constantly getting out her cell phone and looking at the display where it might say, "Missed call" because she is a mom. She just can't quit thinking about that baby. You can't distract her enough to get him off her mind. She is a mom and that is what moms do. All you need for a dad is a good baseball game and he will completely forget about the baby, but moms, moms are different. They are un-distractable.

Now, this next question has a bit of a built-in theological problem, but hang with me here. What do you think God thinks about in idle moments? When He has nothing to do or He is waiting in line, where does the mind of the Almighty drift?

This has a built-in theological problem in that God can think about everything all the time. Your mind will drift in and out as you read this book, wondering where I am going with this, or wandering to think about something else entirely. But, God can track with you all the time. He can think every thought that any human will ever think and he can think about all of those things all the time—simultaneously. Now, that is bandwidth, and God has unlimited bandwidth.

But we get some insight into this question when Jesus told us not one, not two, but three back to back stories to make the same point. Jesus is really emphasizing something here through his repetition.

The first one goes like this:

Suppose one of you has a hundred sheep and loses one of them. Does he not leave the ninety-nine in the open country and go after the lost sheep until he finds it? Luke 15:4 (NIV)

When we hear that word, "lost," in church, or in a Christian book, we think immediately about a theological category. But, when Jesus used the word, it was just an ordinary word. It wasn't a religious word at all. It was just a normal word.

So, I want to invite you to think about how we use that word, lost, in ordinary contexts.

I think of a time when I was traveling on the West Coast. We had spent the day at Universal Studios. As I left the park, I stopped to buy some gifts for the kids. I pulled out my credit card to make the purchase. I drove across town and stopped at a restaurant near our hotel. When I pulled out the credit card to pay for the meal, I noticed the credit card I had used to pay for the gifts at Universal Studios was lost. I keep my credit cards in a particular place in my wallet, so I could tell immediately we had a problem. I looked through the pile of loyalty cards I have in another place in my wallet, and by this time I was panicking. After rummaging through all my cards several times, I had to come to the conclusion that my credit card was lost.

Lost, think about that word lost.

If you had been enjoying dinner with us that night, you would have found me to be more than a little focused. You would have found me to be almost obsessed. If you had said to me, "Don't worry about it. You are on vacation. You need to relax. I am sure there will be no abuse. Enjoy your vacation. Deal with it when you get home."

I would have responded with a panic. You would have heard a tone. "Don't tell me not to worry about it. We are going to worry about this and worry about this right now. I am going to look up the number for the credit card. I am going to call them right now. I am going to have them look up the number for the credit card. I am going to have them check and see if there has been any abuse. If there has, I am going to contest that. In any case, I am going to have them shut down this card and issue me a new one with a new number. And, we are going to deal with this right now before dessert comes." I was rather focused. Something dear to us that is lost does that to us.

And Jesus is telling us something about the heart of God in these three parables. God is a little bit the way we are when we lose something. He is kind of focused in on that which is lost. He can think about everything all the time, but he doesn't. He is focused in on that which is lost.

A lost coin

Jesus told us not one parable, not two parables, but three parables to illustrate and emphasize this same point. The second went like this.
Or suppose a woman has ten silver coins and loses one. Does she not light a lamp, sweep the house and search carefully until she finds it? Luke 15:8 (NIV)

When I was growing up, I was constantly getting lost. I have included a picture of me when I was about a year old. You can see that I am on a leash, like you might put on a dog. This might seem a little cruel to me, but my parents thought it more humane than letting me do what I was prone to do, and that was wander off and get lost. I was the last of four kids, my parents were missionaries and we were constantly traveling. I had been around the world a time and a half by the time I was a year and a half old.

When I was five we were furloughing in Fort Worth, Texas. The shopping is not so great in the Philippines, so my parents had gone over to Town East Mall in East Dallas to enjoy some first-class American shopping. It is a huge mall, even by today's standards and back then, it was an eye-popping moment for some missionaries from the back woods of the Philippines.

My dad was watching me. You can be sure that is true, because this would never happen to a Mom. Suddenly, my dad looked around and I was lost. He circled around to find me and made a bigger circle and a bigger circle and a bigger circle and next thing you know he bumped into my mom and had to come clean with her about the fact that he had hadn't seen me in a while and I was lost.

Well, what did they do? If you had spoken to my mom in that moment and said to her, "Don't worry about it. You have three other kids. Worst case scenario, you can make more." You would have found her to be rather focused with the focus that we get when something that is dear to us is lost. You would have heard her say, "Don't tell me not to worry about it, we are going to worry. We are going to worry and we are going to worry right now. We are going to look in shops, and behind racks and watch for any suspicious looking characters and call the security and look and look and look and keep looking till my boy is found." You would have found my mom to be rather focused. You might have said she is almost obsessed. When something that is dear to us is lost, it does that to us.

When Jesus told us this story, he was telling us something about the heart of God.

This seems a rather obvious point to me, but they did eventually find me. I was asleep on one of the park-style benches in the mall.

Jesus told us not one parable, not two parables, but three parables to make this point. The third one went like this. There was a boy. He wanted his inheritance and he didn't want to wait. He asked, and, unbelievably, the dad said yes. He wrote him a check. I picture the boy running off to Las Vegas, Nevada and spending his wad of cash on wine, women, song, seafood buffets, gambling and Celine Dion tickets. After a while, he runs out of money, he comes to his senses and heads home. Note this verse:

But while he was still a long way off, his father saw him and was filled with compassion for him; he ran to his son, threw his arms around him and kissed him. Luke 15:20 (NIV)

What does this tell you the father had been doing over the last several years? Had he just gone on with his life? No. He spent a lot of time walking back and forth across that porch and praying for that boy and scanning the horizon and obsessing about the boy who was lost. When something is lost it does that to us, and Jesus is telling us something about the heart of the Father: he is more than a little focused on that which is lost.

Let me invite you to underline this line from Ortberg's message:

It is impossible for us to love the Father without sharing His heart for those who are far from Him.

Many people think they are growing spiritually because they are attending church and doing Bible Studies and singing songs and learning Bible doctrine, but their heart is not growing more and more like the heart of the Father who is rather focused on those who are lost.

Some in the business world are diligently working at climbing the ladder of success only to discover that the ladder is leaning against the wrong wall. Many in the church are climbing the ladder, rung after rung, only to discover that the ladder is leaning against the wrong wall. It is not against the wall of closeness to the true God. It is against the wall of religiosity. In many cases, we are not becoming more Christlike, we are only becoming more churchy.

The example of Jesus

Jesus was farther up the mountain of spiritual maturity than any man who has ever lived. In fact, He is at the top of the mountain of spiritual maturity. And what was Jesus all about? The scripture says in one place, "For the Son of Man came to seek and to save what was lost." Luke 19:10 (NIV) Luke summarizes Jesus' life by concluding that he was all about going after people who are far from God.

In another place, Luke records, "The Son of Man came eating and drinking, and you say, 'Here is a glutton and a drunkard, a friend of tax collectors and 'sinners.'" Luke 7:34. Drop Jesus in a crowd somewhere and he would not drift in the direction of religious people. The drift of Jesus' life was in the direction of people who are far from God.

Here is one more: "Jesus answered them, 'It is not the healthy who need a doctor, but the sick. I have not come to call the righteous, but sinners to repentance.'" Luke 5:31-32. This most spiritually mature person was all about going after people who are far from God.

God would do that work in our life. Fundamentally what God is trying to do in our lives is to make us like Jesus. And what Jesus was all about was going after people who are far from God. Many of us think we are growing spiritually because we engage in religious activity, but our heart is not getting more and more like the heart of Jesus.

Not mere indifference

Some think they are growing spiritually even though their heart is not growing more and more like the heart of God. They are rather indifferent to people who are far from God.

But, for others, it is no mere indifference. It is actual preference. Some actually prefer not to be around sinners.

In some cases, the reason is pretty simple. Some people are kind of hard to love. (This is true of people who are far from God, as well as Christian people.)

I have done a home Bible Study over the last several years. There was a guy coming to my study for a time who lives at the Gospel Rescue Mission. I don't think he takes a shower every day. He wears a T-shirt that does not completely cover his belly. He is not a very interesting conversationalist. He wants to talk mostly about himself and his problems, and, honestly, the same old problems.

The Bible study went from 7.00 p.m. to about 8.30 p.m. One night, we had gone out to eat before the study, planning to be back about 6.30. At 6.15 my cell phone rings. It is my son, "Jim is here." I rush home to greet him. That same night, about 45 minutes into the Bible Study Jim hops up and starts walking out. I thought maybe we had said something to make him mad. I stopped the Bible Study and said, "Uh, Jim, is everything O.K.?" ""Yeah, everything is fine, I just needed to leave early tonight." "Oh, well, O.K. Hope to see you next time." Quite honestly, the guy is kind of weird.

I have found myself thinking at times, "I hope Jim doesn't show up for Bible study tonight."

I wonder if I am the only one capable of that kind of thought. And I wonder, if you are capable of that kind of thinking, if you would join me in repenting of that kind of thinking. Because when we entertain that kind of thinking, we show our hearts to be very far from the heart of God.

I spoke on this once in North Carolina. I had a lady come up to me afterwards and say to me, "You are darn right I don't like being around sinners. They smoke and they smell like they have been smoking. They drink and they act like they have been drinking. They curse. They use foul language. Their jokes are all tainted with sexual overtones. They are materialistic and worldly and I don't like being around them."

On one level, I understand that. But I have to wonder, is there any surprise that they don't like coming to our churches? Do you think they can sense that? Do you like being in places where people don't like you? I don't, and I don't think they do either. And it is impossible to escape the conclusion that the work God is trying to do in our lives is to make us focused in on those who are lost, like we are focused when we lose our keys. It is impossible to escape the conclusion that the Father gave up the life of his Son so he could be close to people like that.

Is it good or bad?

Some are indifferent to people who are far from God. For some it is not mere indifference, it is actual preference. And some think this preference is a sign of their maturity.

It was true of the Pharisees. They counted as one of the great marks of their maturity this tendency they had to not be around sinners. Jesus counted it as the greatest sign of the fact that they had missed it.

It was true of me. I began getting very serous about my faith in my High School years. Late in my High School years I began to think about college. I thought, "You know, I am tired of being around the sinners at my High School. I am tired of the drinking and the jokes and the smoking and the rudeness and the crudeness and the worldliness. I want to go to a Christian college where there are Christian students and I want to get away for all this ungodliness."

And, I think if you had asked me, I think I would have said that this is a sign that I get it. I am not like the other kids in my youth group, many of who are half-hearted or uncommitted. It doesn't bother them to be around the worldliness at our High School. It doesn't bother them because they pretty much fit right in. But I am serious about my faith. I get it. I am committed. And the proof of the fact that I get it is the fact that I am selecting a Christian college so I can get away from all these sinners.

Looking back, I have to say it is proof that I did not get it. The work God is doing in our lives is that he is trying to make us move toward, not away from sinners.

Huts of Refuge

The most compelling story I have heard in years was a story John Ortberg told in the middle of this message. In fact, he named the message after this story. Allow me to quote in John's own words.

Several years ago we took a vacation and we went to Massachusetts and we visited a little museum on Nantucket Island. It was devoted to a volunteer organization that was formed centuries ago, over 300 years ago.

In those days, travel by sea was extremely dangerous, and given storms in the Atlantic, and the real rocky coasts of

Massachusetts, many lives were lost real close to the shore, within a mile or less of the land.

And a group of people who lived on that island couldn't stand to think about all these people going down so close to them. So, they went into the life saving business. They banded together to form what was originally was called the Humane Society. We think about animals with that name now, but in those days, that was a life saving deal for them. They built little huts that dotted the shore. You can still see one of them in this museum. They built little huts containing boats and rescue equipment. They were sometimes called huts of refuge.

Huts of refuge. And people were posted in those huts all the time. And their job was just to keep watching the sea. And any time a ship went down, the word would go out. They would devote everything. They would risk themselves to save every life they could. Twenty four hours a day, seven days a week, somebody was watching. Everybody was willing.
They did it for no money. They did it for no recognition. They did it just because they prized human life.

And to remind them how seriously they took this task, and what was at stake, they adopted a motto. I love this motto: "You have to go out, but you don't have to come back." That is a catchy little recruiting slogan, don't you think? "You have to go out, but you don't have to come back." You wouldn't think that would entice a whole lot of people into joining them, but it did.

It is a fascinating thing to read accounts in that museum of people who risked everything, even their lives, to save other people they had never met, faces they had never seen, names they might not ever know.

Over time things changed and after a while, what would come to be known as the U.S. Coast guard, started to take over this task. And, for a little while, the Coast Guard and the Life Saving Society worked side by side. Eventually the idea that carried the day was, "Let the professionals do it. They are better trained. They get paid for it."

Volunteers stopped manning the little huts. They stopped searching the coastline for sinking ships. They stopped sending out teams to rescue people.

And, it is a funny thing. They couldn't bring themselves to disband. And the Life Saving society still exists today. It meets every once in a while in Boston or someplace in New England to have dinners. And they hand out awards for things like community service. They enjoy each other's company. They sponsor programs. They get together. They are just not in the life saving business any more. They don't scour the coastline anymore to see if anybody is going down.

They don't know the thrill any more of what it is to risk themselves to save a life that could perish. They don't speak those words to each other any more, "You have to go out, but you don't have to come back." They are just not in the life-saving business anymore.

It happens all the time. It doesn't happen in a day. It doesn't happen in a month. But over time, a church forgets it is in the life saving business. It usually doesn't disband, at least not until much later. People still meet. They still enjoy each other's company. They still use words like community. They still have services and buildings and staffs and programs. They might even be involved in various forms of community service. They are just not sending out teams any more for people who are going down. They are just not really scouring neighborhoods and offices, schools and networks and cities to see if there is somebody that needs to be saved.

They forgot, maybe, that Jesus put this rescue effort in the hands of volunteers who would love the people that God loves so much and adopt for themselves the motto, "You have to go out, but you don't have to come back."

They have buildings and budgets and staffs and meetings. They are just not in the life saving business any more. It can happen to a church. It can happen to a small group. It can happen to an individual. And don't think it can't happen in your church; don't think it can't. Don't think it can't happen to you.

Whether or not we stay into the life-saving business is in the hands of the people in this room. Jesus is still looking for people who are willing to go into the life-saving business. That is what the church does.

So let me ask you: where is your heart toward people who are far from God. We can reach them by giving Friday Nights to Jesus. My question is, do you want to?

The Psychology of Influence

For years I have tried to understand the incredible power of giving Friday nights to Jesus. We have looked at the biblical admonition to "offer hospitality without grumbling," and "Get in the habit of inviting guests home for dinner". We have looked at the sociological data on the epidemic of loneliness in our country. We have seen the incredible effectiveness in giving Friday nights to Jesus in real life situations. I'd like to turn now to some psychological data to understand the power of this simple tool.

Robert Cialdini, Ph.D. has written an incredible book entitled *The Psychology of Influence.* I consider it a classic, and so do a lot of other people:

- Amazon's editorial review said, "Arguably the best book ever on what is increasingly becoming the science of persuasion."
- David Myers said, "The most informative and engaging book ever written on the weapons of influence."
- From the back cover: *Influence* has clearly established itself as the most important book on persuasion ever published.

Cialdini outlines six psychological principles of influence. I'd like to summarize each of these, and then speak briefly to how giving Friday nights to Jesus relates to each.

Reciprocation

The Law of Reciprocation states: do unto others and they tend to do unto you. We seem bound by an internal law to keep the score even. When people do for us, we just must do for them.

A few years ago, a University professor tried a little experiment. He sent Christmas cards to a sampling of perfect strangers. Although he expected some reaction, the response was amazing. Christmas cards started pouring in from all over the country. This is the power of reciprocation. When we do for people, they tend to want to do for us.

Kurt Mortensen affirms the power of reciprocity in his book, *Maximum Influence.* He tells the story of a German soldier in World War I. He was given the assignment of sneaking behind enemy lines, capturing and questioning enemy soldiers. He came upon one such soldier eating his lunch. The startled soldier did not know what to do, and, in his stress, offered the German soldier a piece of bread. The German soldier took it, but then couldn't bring himself to capture this man who had just been generous enough to share his lunch with him. He let him go. That is the power of reciprocity.

It could be argued that some of the principles of influence border on manipulation. If we offer hospitality to people and create a sense of obligation in them to come to our church, are we manipulating them? Where is the line between manipulation and persuasion? Webster defines manipulation as, "to change by artful or unfair means so as to serve one's purpose." Using this definition, I would say that giving Friday nights to Jesus is not manipulation. It is not unfair to offer hospitality and if people respond by becoming our friend and getting involved in our church and coming to love our Lord, all the better. Everyone wins.

They win because they have some new friends, a new relationship with Christ, the hope of eternal life. All of life is better. You win because you have some new friends and you get the feeling of being used by God to expand the kingdom. Your church wins because this is an effective means of outreach and many can be added to your church. God wins because he loves it when the lost are redeemed. Everybody wins.

No one feels cheated. No one feels used. No one feels manipulated. Everyone wins.

When we do nice things for people, it warms their heart. They tend to want to listen to what we have to say. Their heart opens up to the message of the gospel.

Servant evangelism does a similar things. Steve Sjogren has found that as we are obedient to the command of God to offer a cup of cold water in Jesus name, people tend to warm up to the message about Jesus. Modern equivalents of a cup of cold water include free car washes and free gift wrapping at Christmas time. Serving people has a predictable effect of opening their heart to us whether it is a cup of cold water or coffee cake and Diet Coke on Friday night. (See www.servantevangelism.com)

Commitment and Consistency

People have an incredible desire to be consistent. We hate what psychologists call cognitive dissonance—that feeling that I am inconsistent with my own values. People will do almost anything to resolve the dissonance—even to their own detriment.

I ran face to face with this law as a child. I was an incredibly picky eater as a child and extremely stubborn about it. I survived pretty much on starches–pasta and potatoes. My parents tried to push me outside of my comfort zone to try other foods, but not without a fight.

One day, they tried to push me to eat a cream puff. It was new, foreign, unheard of, and I would have nothing of it. "No! No! No!" I clenched my teeth together in refusal to try this new treat. My parents insisted. I am not sure why it was this choice that made them go to the mat and want to win this one, but they were determined to poke at least one bite of this treat into my mouth no matter what. Eventually they prevailed and pried apart my teeth wide enough to get a small bite of cream puff in.

It was delicious. Mouth-watering, delectable, luscious, scrumptious, tasty, I-want-some-more-now, yummy. Any guesses as to what I did next after my parents poked this mouth-watering morsel past my teeth? "Yuck! I hate it!" I spit it out. But, I was found sneaking into the kitchen later and squirreling away my own private stash of cream puff. This is the law of consistency. I had gone on public record to declare for all the world to hear, "I hate cream puffs!" and I wouldn't let the creamy texture or sweet taste keep me from my consistency.

People go to incredible lengths to maintain consistency. In one experiment, scientists staged a robbery five feet from a stranger relaxing on the beach. Only 20% said something when a thief came by and stole a radio. Most people just didn't want to get involved. But, with one tweak, this number shot up to 95%. Before the radio owner walked off, they made a simple request, "Would you keep an eye on my stuff?" Everyone said, "yes" and 95% of them were consistent with their commitment.

In the context of a friendly evening of game playing and snacks, it is easy enough to say, "You think you could join us in our Bible Study this weekend?" You don't want to say, "No." These people have been kind enough to have you over for an evening of fun. They have treated you as a friend. You agree. Because of the law of consistency, you will tend to comply with what you said you would do. Do they always do what they say they will do? Of course not. But, it is a powerful source of influence. People tend to do what they say they will do.

Scarcity

People are motivated to get what they can't get. They are attracted to the scarce. This is why stores make limited time offers–they want to make it seem scarce. It is why a saleslady in a jewelry story said to my wife yesterday, "If you purchase these right now, I will not charge you any tax." Right now. If you wait till later, the offer may go away. It is limited.

Collections of trading cards, coins, beany babies or stamps are valuable because they are rare. Some flawed items are especially valuable because they are rare–blurred stamps and dollar bills without a serial number are two examples. The rare flaw makes them scarce, and thus, valuable.

One Virginia-based study researched the affect of scarcity on children as young as 2 years old. As it turns out, this tendency starts young. Children wanted an unavailable toy that was behind Plexiglas more than they wanted the available toy. Every parent knows this. Send two kids into a room full of toys. Wait till one child picks out one toy to play with. I will give you ten to one odds that the other child will want that same toy. Why? It is the one toy that was unavailable, and thus, scarce.

Come to think of it, this tendency goes all the way back to the beginning. What was it that made the forbidden apple so delectable? Was it, perhaps, that it was the one fruit that was off-limits and thus scarce?

This is the very problem with church. It is not scarce. It happens every seven days. If I miss this week, I can come back next week. Some churches try combat this by emphasizing certain guest speakers, certain musical performances or certain sermon series. Although church will still be here next month, this series, this musician, this event won't be.

This is one thing that makes giving Friday nights for Jesus so attractive. It is not everyday someone gets an invitation to go to a friends house for dinner. For many, it has been a long time since they have had such an invitation. It is scarce, and as such, valuable.

Sometimes, the scarcity principle can cause unintended affects. One Colorado study revealed that teenagers who were forbidden to contact a particular member of the opposite sex actually found them more attractive. We all want what we can't have. It is scarce, and thus valuable.

Dade county (Miami), Florida was concerned about the environmental impact of phosphate in soap products, so, they did what government does: they passed a law banning the sale or possession of phosphate soap products. The result? People went to neighboring counties to purchase the soap and hoarded it in their pantries.

We all want what is rare or scarce and we all know that one of the rarest things of all is a friend. Thus, when someone treats us like a friend, we recognize it as a rare thing and we respond with open arms.

Authority

Most evangelism training programs assume that the normal way for someone to come to faith in Christ is through an individual sharing their faith with them. Although individual friends and family members have a huge impact on people's decision to accept Christ, most people don't accept Christ when a friend witnesses to them. Most people accept Christ under the influence of a recognized authority like a preacher or evangelist. People are influenced to come to church with their friends, or, because a friend invites them. But, they prefer to hear and respond to the gospel message not from a friend, but from an authority.

You can check out the validity of this statement yourself, as I have on many occasions. I have asked a number of groups how they came to faith in Christ:

21. Under the influence of their parents or family member.
22. By themselves.
23. Under the influence of an individual, but not a family member.
24. Under the influence of a preacher in a worship service or evangelistic crusade.

I was actually only interested in responses 3 and 4, because responses 1 and 2 don't have a lot of evangelistic potential. Most witnessing training assumes that #3 is a common scenario. I found that not to be the case. The vast majority of the people I have interviewed came to faith in Christ in a public meeting under the influence of an authority figure–a pastor or evangelist.

This finding fits nicely with the findings of Cialdini who discovered that we are strongly influenced by the presence of authority. There is a tendency to think that people are rebellious and want to go against authority. Some do. But, most drive the speed limit, obey the rules, do as they are told. Not all, but most do.

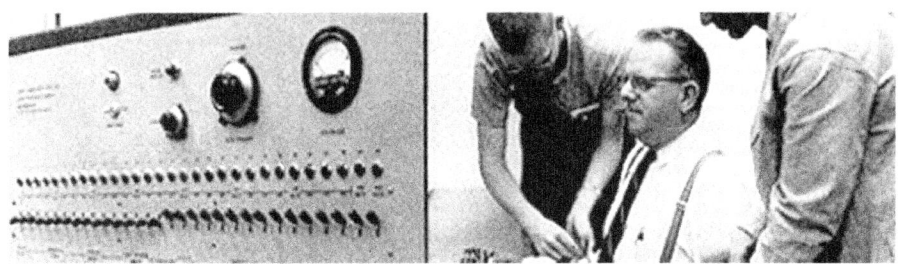

Advertising uses this psychological principle constantly with phrases like "experts agree," and "rated #1." They site references to studies done by experts in their field. These authorities validate the claim that their product is the best product.

The most chilling example of this tendency to follow authority was in an experiment conducted by Professor Stanley Milgram of Yale University between 1961 - 1962.

This was the aftermath of the Holocaust and everyone was asking, "How could anyone do these things to another human being?" Milgram wanted to find out the effect that authority had on the question.

He placed an ad asking for volunteers to take part in a memory test. The volunteer is introduced to a stern looking man in a white lab coat. The man carries a clip board and looks very "official." He is also introduced to another volunteer. The experimenter explains that the experiment is designed to reveal the effects of punishment in learning.

One volunteer is assigned the role of teacher, while the other is assigned the role of student. The student is strapped to a chair to prevent him from moving and electrodes are placed under his arm. The teacher is asked to read a list of two word pairs, and the student is asked to read them back. If the student gets the answer wrong, the teacher is to shock him with a series of electric shocks, starting with 15 volts and working up to a stunning 450 volts.

This is all a ruse. There is no real shock at all. The test is not about memory and pain, it is about obedience to authority. The student is an actor. Each time he gets an answer wrong, the teacher shocks him with steadily increasing pulses of electricity. The student writhes in pain, begging to be released. The teacher is told that it is very important that he continue as the accuracy of the test will be in jeopardy if he does not.

Before he conducted the study, Milgram sent a description of the study to a number of colleagues, graduate students, and psychology majors at Yale. People estimated that only 1% to 2% of the subjects would take the shocks all the way up to the 450 volt level.

The actual results: two thirds followed the man in the white lab coat all the way up to the 450 volt level. At this point, the subject was writhing and begging and pleading to be let out. Not one stopped before shocking their subject with 300 volts. Not one.

(If you are curious about this, do a search on the Internet for The Milgram Study. I found actual audio clips of the students in the study pleading to be released. Authority is a powerful thing.)

What is the lesson for us and evangelism? Most people prefer to respond to Christ by responding to an authority figure such as a pastor or evangelist. This is the way most people come to faith in Christ, yet, much of our evangelism training is rooted in a different model.

Evangelism works best as a team. Ordinary laymen have people into their home. They love them in common, ordinary, pedestrian ways. They befriend them until their friends warm up to a message about what a friend they can have in Jesus. We love them and their heart warms up to a message about a God who loves them. This message could be delivered by the friend, or, it could be delivered by an authority figure.

This is not the only way, but it is the most common way that most people seem to prefer to come to faith in Christ.

There are two more principles of influence in Cialdini's book. These two are the most powerful in terms of explaining the effectiveness of the ministry of hospitality.

Liking

People like to buy from people they like. We like to buy insurance from people we like. We like to buy cars from people we like. It would be a little crass to say we like to buy religion from people we like. Perhaps better to say we are most influenced spiritually by people we like.

People refuse to buy from people they don't like. Haven't you ever refused a purchase from a pushy or obnoxious salesman, even though it was a good deal?

Instinctively we know this to be true. Cialdini provides the hard research to validate our gut instinct. Further, he explains why we like some people and dislike others.

Salesmen cash in on the formula of liking and none more than Joe Girard. For 12 years straight, he won the record for the "#1 Car Salesman," selling five cars every day he worked. He was called "the world's greatest car salesman" by the Guinness Book of World Record.

Joe Girard's formula is simple: a likeable personality and a fair price.

But, what exactly is a likeable personality? Cialdini's research uncovered

- **Physical attractiveness.** We tend to like pretty people. We tend to assign good looking people favorable characteristics such as talent, kindness, honesty and intelligence. Research into court cases reveals that better looking defendants are found not-guilty less often. When they are found guilty, they tend to serve less time.

Lesson: obviously we can't do too much about certain physical features. However, we can make the best with what we have. We can do what we can to make ourselves and our homes as attractive as possible.

- **Similarity**. People tend to like people like themselves. People like people who dress like them, talk like them, act like them.

Lesson: we would do well to find common ground. Life is complex. Look for the things you have in common.

- **Compliments.** People like people who like them, or, who say nice things about them. Joe Girard used to send cards that said simply, "I like you." People like being liked and they made Joe the world's greatest car salesman.

Lesson: find something to *sincerely* compliment.

- **Contact and Cooperation.** There is a tendency to love the familiar. We tend to root for the home team. We like what we know. All other things being equal, we will grow to like people more as we spend more time with them. A Milwaukee study revealed that people tend to prefer a reverse image of themselves–the image you see in the mirror, while their friends prefer looking at the true image. Both parties prefer seeing the familiar.

Lesson: This law helps to explain why hospitality works. It makes us familiar. This assumes, of course, that we are not somehow irritating people in the process. And, it can be overdone, as the Proverbs teach: "Seldom set foot in your neighbor's house–too much of you, and he will hate you." Proverbs 25:17 (NIV)

- **Conditioning and Association.** We tend to like people who are with people we like. We tend to like people if we associate having a good time with them. We tend to like people if the things we did with them were fun, or brought us pleasure.

Lesson: we ought to work hard at making the events we invite people to are fun, relaxing and positive. If we are doing a "Dinner and a movie," tell them what the movie is ahead of time. Better that they stay home than endure a chick-flick if they hate chick-flicks. The evening is not about us. It is about them. Pay attention to them and make sure that they are having a good time. Include them in everything. If they have a bummer time, the association will do more harm than good.

Summary: We are influenced by people we like. We tend to like people who . . .
- Look their best
- Have something in common with us
- Compliment us
- Spend time with us and are familiar to us
- Remind us of pleasant associations

The last point of Cialdini's finding is the most powerful.

Social proof

We tend to think that only teenagers and children succumb to peer pressure (social proof) but the hard research indicates otherwise. People tend to do what the people around them do. If the people are around them go to church, they go to church. If the people around them believe, they believe. If the people around them drink and swear and curse and chew, they drink and swear and curse and chew. People–all people–are incredibly influenced by the people around them.

People like to buy the popular brands. Best-selling is a kind of short cut for "best." If all those people like it, it can't be so bad, can it? They can't all be dummies. On the other hand, if no one else thinks it is good, it must not be that good. People–all people– are incredibly influenced by the people around them.

People laugh more when the show includes canned laughter. Shuttle drivers will get more tips if they start the day with a few dollar bills of their own that look like tips left by other people. "Well, others left a tip, so it must be appropriate to tip." Billy Graham has counselors walk forward to give the appearance that if you walk forward, you are not alone. No one wants to be alone.

Psychologist Albert Bandura discovered that children who were terrified of dogs were substantially relieved of their paranoia when they watched other children happily playing with dogs for twenty minutes a day. After only four days, 67% of the formerly terrified children were willing to crawl into a playpen with dogs. They were willing to happily stay with dogs, petting and scratching them, even when everyone else left the room. They did follow up tests a month later. The positive change persisted. Later studies revealed that the children did not even have to watch live children watching real dogs–children on film would do the trick.

Kurt Mortensen found further evidence for social proof and included it in his book *Maximum Influence.* For example, Professor Kirk Hansen of the Stanford Business School demonstrated that when he boosted downloads for files on the web, those files received higher downloads.

In another study, participants were asked to say which of two lines on a screen was longest. One was clearly longer than the other. People were seeded into the audience to give the wrong answer; 75% of the participants gave the wrong answer at least once.

A New York City study showed that if a group of people were looking up into the sky, passerby strangers would also look up. The more people there were looking up, the higher the percentage of passersby looking up.

A macabre example of social proof can be found in the murder of Catherine Genovese. The New York Times ran the story in March 1964.

"For more than half an hour 38 respectable, law-abiding citizens in Queens watched a killer stalk and stab a woman in three separate attacks in Kew Gardens.

"Miss Genovese screamed: 'Oh, my God, he stabbed me! Please help me! Please help me!'"

"Twice the sound of their voices and the sudden glow of their bedroom lights interrupted him and frightened him off. Each time he returned, sought her out and stabbed her again. Not one person telephoned the police during the assault; one witness called after the woman was dead."

Social scientists searched and searched for answers to how a society could become so cold, so uncaring, so heartless, so mean. The most passable explanation: social proof. All thirty-eight of the people could see the other thirty-seven. All of us, in a situation like that, are not certain what to do. Should we act and risk getting hurt ourselves, or do we let this woman suffer? Should we put our own life on the line to help a stranger, perhaps trying in vain? In the moment of indecision we look around for clues as to what is appropriate behavior. When we see thirty seven other people not acting, we tend to not act either. Most people don't want to stick out from the crowd.

Conclusion

What difference does all this make to those of us who would spread the gospel? Simple. If we will be their friend, people will tend to do what their friends do. We just have to change their friends first. When we become their frame of reference socially, we become a dominant influence in their lives. If we are strangers, they can easily resist that message.

We have known this forever. Relationships are the key to evangelism. What is new? What is new is a way to make relationships systematic, consistent, calendar-able. If we can make it something we can put on our calendar, we make it something we can do. Many of us are responsible, committed, caring Christians. If we make relationship evangelism something within our reach, something we can schedule into our lives we will do it. If we can reduce it to something we can put on a to-do list, something we can enter into our PDA, we will get it done.

But lifestyle, or relationship has always been so nebulous. It has always been so slippery. When do you get around to doing this lifestyle, relationship, feel-good thing? Well, "all the time," some say. Well, "all the time" translates into good intentions that don't get done. They don't get done because they don't get on the calendar and on the to-do list and an already crowded calendar and to-do list crowds them out.

What is the solution? Give Friday night to Jesus. An informal time of Diet Coke, table games, and coffee cake can make all the difference. One night really can make all the difference. And, it doesn't have to be Friday night. But, it does have to be some night that shows up on a to-do list and a calendar.

Try it, will you? I close with this challenge: try it for three months. Every week give Friday night (or Sunday lunch or Sunday night) to Jesus. Invite some friends over. Invite some people who are far from God over. Perhaps some prospects to your Sunday School class or home group. Perhaps some members who are wandering from God and from church. Perhaps some friends, neighbors or work associates that need love. Do it every week for three months. It will refresh your life, revitalize your church, and reach your world.

Epilogue

I have told you a number of my stories about how parties have made a difference. I have saved my best story for last. It is actually not my story. It is told by Tony Compolo and is incredible. I have saved the best for last.

A party for a prostitute

I was in Honolulu with jet lag and awake at 3:30 a.m. wandering up and down the streets looking for a place to get something to eat. Up a side street I found one of those sleazy places that deserves the name "greasy spoon", but it was the only place I could find. I asked for a cup of coffee and a donut. As I sat munching my donut, the door of the diner suddenly opened and to my discomfort in marched 8 or 9 provocative and boisterous prostitutes. Since it was a small place they sat on either side of me. Their talk was loud and crude and I felt totally out of place. I was about to make my getaway when I overheard the woman sitting beside me say: "Tomorrow's my birthday. I am going to be 39."

Her friend responded in a nasty tone, " So what do you want from me? A birthday party? What do you want: Do you want me to get you a cake and sing 'happy birthday'?"

"Come on," said the woman sitting next to me,

"Why do you have to be so mean? I was just telling you, that's all. Why do you have to put me down? I was just telling you it was my birthday. I don't want anything from you. I mean, why should you give me a birthday party? I've never had a birthday party in my whole life. Why should I want one now?"

When I heard that, I made a decision. I sat and waited until the women had left then I called over the guy behind the counter and asked, "Do they come in here every night?

"Yeah!" he answered.

"The one right next to me, does she come here every night?

"Yeah" he said. That's Agnes, Yeah, she comes every night. Why'd'ya want to know?"

"Because I heard her say that tomorrow is her birthday." I told him... "What do you say you and I do something about that? What do you think about us throwing a birthday party for her - right here - tomorrow night?"

A cute smile slowly crossed his chubby cheeks and he answered with measured delight, "That's great! I like it. It's a great idea." Calling to his wife, who did the cooking in the back room, he shouted, "Hey! come out here. This guy's got a great idea. Tomorrow's Agnes's birthday. This guy wants us to go in with him and throw a birthday party for her -- right here -- tomorrow night."

His wife came out of the back room all bright and smiley. She said, "That's a wonderful idea. You know Agnes is one of those people who is really nice and kind and nobody ever does anything nice and kind for her.".

"Look," I told them, "if it's ok with you, I'll get back here tomorrow morning about 2:30 and decorate the place. I'll even get a birthday cake!"

"No way," said Harry (that was his name) "The birthday cake is my thing. I'll make the cake.

At 2:30 the next morning, I was back at the diner. I had picked up some crepe-paper decorations at the store and had made a sign out of a big piece of soft cardboard that read, "Happy Birthday, Agnes." I decorated the diner from one end to the other. I had that diner looking good.

The woman who did the cooking must have gotten the word out on the street, because by 3:15 every prostitute in Honolulu was in the place. It was wall-to-wall prostitutes... and me!

At 3:30 on the dot, the door of the diner swung open and in came Agnes and her friend. I had everybody ready (after all, I was kind of the M.C. of the affair) and when they came in we all screamed, "Happy Birthday!"

Never have I seen a person so flabbergasted ... so stunned... so shaken. Her mouth fell open. Her legs seemed to buckle a bit. Her friend grabbed her arm to steady her. As she was led to sit on one of the stools along the counter, we all sang "Happy Birthday" to her. As we came to the end of our singing, her eyes moistened. Then, when the birthday cake and all the candles were carried out, she lost it and just openly cried.

Harry gruffly mumbled, "Blow out the candles, Agnes, Come on! Blow out the candles. If you don't blow out the candles, I'm gonna blow out the candles!" And, after an endless few seconds, she did. Then he handed her a knife and told her, "Cut the cake, Agnes, Yo, Agnes, we all want some cake."

Agnes looked down at the cake. Then without taking her eyes off it, she slowly and softly said, "Look , Harry, is it all right with you if I... I mean is it O.K. if I kind of... what I want to ask you is ... is it O.K. if I keep the cake a little while. I mean is it all right if we don't eat it right away?"

Harry shrugged and answered, "Sure! It's O.K.! If you want to keep it, keep the cake. Take it home if you want." "Can I?" she asked. Then, looking at me she said, "I live just down the street a couple of doors. I want to take the cake home, O.K.? I'll be right back. Honest!"

She got off the stool, picked up the cake, and, carrying it like it was the Holy Grail, walked slowly toward the door. As we all just stood there motionless, she left.

When the door closed. There was a stunned silence in the place. Not knowing what else to do, I broke the silence by saying, "What do you say we pray?"

Looking back on it now it seems more than strange for a sociologist to be leading a prayer meeting with a bunch of prostitutes in a diner in Honolulu at 3:30 in the morning, but then it just felt like the right thing to do. I prayed for Agnes. I prayed for her salvation. I prayed that her life would be changed and that God would be good to her. When I finished, Harry leaned over the counter and with a trace of hostility in his voice, he said, "Hey, you never told me you were a preacher. What kind of church do you belong to?"

In one of those moments when just the right words came, I answered, "I belong to a church that throws birthday parties for whores at 3:30 in the morning."

Harry waited a moment and then almost sneered as he answered, "No you don't! There's no church like that. If there was, I'd join it. I'd join a church like that.!"

Wouldn't we all? Wouldn't we all love to join a church that throws birthday parties for whores at 3:30 in the morning?

Well, that's the kind of church that Jesus was born to create! I don't know where we got that other one that's so prim and proper. But anybody who reads the New Testament will discover a Jesus who loved to party with whores and with all kinds of left out people. The publicans and "sinners" loved Him because He partied with them. The lepers of society found in Him someone who would eat and drink with them. And while the solemnly pious could not relate to what He was about, those lonely people who didn't get invited to parties took to Him with excitement.

I am not sure I can tell you there is a world out there saying they would join a church that throws parties for prostitutes in Honolulu at 3.30 a.m. But, there is a world out there that will become very receptive to the message about a God who loves them if you will love them. If you will love them, their heart will warm up to a message about a God who loves them. If you will be their friend, their heart will warm up to a message about what a friend we can have in Jesus.

Give Friday nights to Jesus. It can refresh your life, revitalize your church, and reach your world.

If you enjoyed this book, would you mind leaving a positive review on Amazon?

Josh Hunt
www.joshhunt.com
josh@joshhunt.com

Printed in Great Britain
by Amazon